Jesus, History, and Mount Darwin

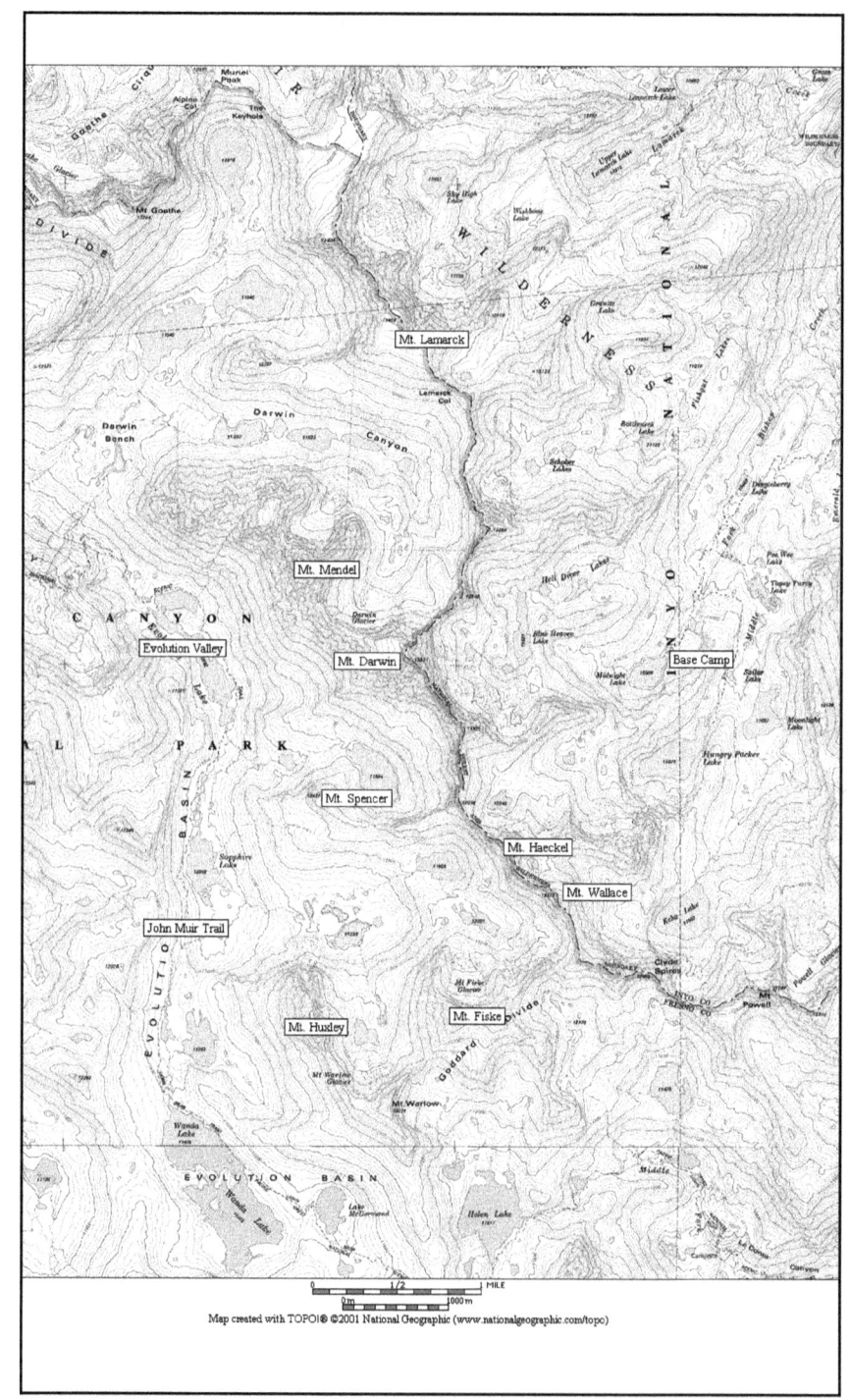

Jesus, History, and Mount Darwin

An Academic Excursion

RICK KENNEDY

WIPF & STOCK · Eugene, Oregon

JESUS, HISTORY, AND MOUNT DARWIN
An Academic Excursion

Copyright © 2008 Rick Kennedy. All rights reserved. Except for brief quotations in critical publications or reviews, no part of this book may be reproduced in any manner without prior written permission from the publisher. Write: Permissions, Wipf and Stock, 199 W. 8th Ave., Suite 3, Eugene, OR 97401.

ISBN 13: 978-1-55635-655-1

Manufactured in the U.S.A.

Also by the author:

A History of Reasonableness: Testimony and Authority in the Art of Thinking (University of Rochester Press, 2004).

Faith at State: A Handbook for Christians at Public Universities (InterVarsity Press, 1995; Wipf & Stock, 2002).

Aristotelian and Cartesian Logic at Harvard: Morton's "System of Logick" and Brattle's "Compendium of Logick" (Colonial Society of Massachusetts, 1995).

Student Notebooks at Colonial Harvard: Manuscripts and Educational Practice, 1650–1740. Co-written and edited with Thomas Knoles and Lucia Zaucha Knoles (American Antiquarian Society, 2003).

Dedicated to

Elizabeth Joy Kennedy
who was too small at the time.

Who can straighten what God has made crooked?
Ecclesiastes 7:13

Consider carefully how you listen.
Luke 8:18

Contents

1 The Plan 1

2 Road Trip 4

3 Base Camp 24

4 Mount Darwin 50

5 Homeward 92

Afterword 105
Bibliography 107

1

The Plan

Back in the 1970s, I learned to love university life. I eventually became a professor of history. I started out a Bible-trusting Christian and have not lost my faith. This book is about the reasonableness of biblical Christianity in universities. By reasonableness, I mean the warranted credibility, if not the persuasiveness, of Christian claims about ancient history. This book is also about Darwinism and natural history. Darwin seems to have lost whatever Christian faith he might have once had, and his ideas about distant natural history are often pitted in classrooms against the more recent ancient history of Christianity. There are many ways people in universities try to get at the tensions between Christianity and Darwinism. Here I want to sidestep most of them. I want to think about two histories, two types of history that can stand side by side even if they are contradictory in many ways. I especially want to sidestep any notions that science is about facts and Christianity about values. Here I treat both as sophisticated systems based on evidence, facts, and inferences. Both use reasonable methods standing within long academic traditions. Both make assertions about what happened in the past.

For Christianity, history is primal. At universities, the struggle with Darwinism is best dealt with at the primal level of history. Darwin was a natural historian proposing that long ago certain things happened—species evolved by a mechanism of variation and selection He then inferred that since the creation of new species did not need God, then it is best to assume that God was not involved.

Christianity is founded on events in human history. St. Paul in 1 Corinthians 15 stakes the truth of Christianity three times on a historical event reported by eyewitnesses. "If Christ has not been raised, our preaching is useless and so is your faith." Again, "If Christ has not been raised your faith is futile." Paul further declares, "You have believed in vain," if you do not believe what is "of first importance: that Christ died for our sins according the scriptures, that he was buried, that he was raised on the third day according to the scriptures." The evidential base upon which to "hold firm" and "stand firm" is the testimony of eyewitnesses: first Peter, then the twelve, then five hundred, then James, then the apostles, then to Paul himself. Peter reminded a group of eyewitnesses in Acts 2 about events as the foundation to Christian revelation: "Listen to this: Jesus of Nazareth was a man accredited by God to you by miracles, wonders and signs, which God did among you through him."

University culture is a Greek culture. "Greeks look for wisdom," Paul noted, "but we preach Christ crucified."[1] What Paul was getting at here is that Greekish philosophy, theology, science, and natural history look for order and try to make sense of things by organizing. Paul wanted to make it clear that God was not to be put in a Greek box. On the other hand, Paul was probably not criticizing Greek historical methods that have affinities with Christianity. Herodotus and Thucydides, the founding fathers of Greek historical writing, were models for Luke and Paul. When it comes to evangelism, Greek methods of history help establish Christ crucified. Greek history accepts the disorderliness of human history in ways that support the disorderliness of history presented in the Bible. In the Bible, God does not create like an engineer. God is not portrayed as a logician whose logic cannot be defeated. God's ways and thoughts are not like the orderly expectations of academic philosophy, theology, science, or natural history. The preacher says: "Who can straighten what God has made crooked?"[2] The academic study of human history is the study of crookedness, of things not going as logic would demand. Jesus is part of that crookedness.

I here apologize for the rest of this book. The goal is grand but the framework is small. Polybius, one of the Greek founders of the discipline of writing human history, ridiculed historians who only haunt libraries and are unwilling to travel to where they can survey the scene of events.[3] I had read Darwin's books, but wanted to survey the scene of Darwin's life. I would have liked to have gone to Darwin's house and to have seen his desk and garden. Better yet, I would have liked to have sailed through

---

1. 1 Cor 1:15–20.
2. Eccl 7:13.
3. Polybius, *Rise of the Roman Empire*, XII, 25e–i.

The Plan

the Beagle Strait at the tip of South America north to the Galapagos. But, given the confines of my life, I decided that the best I could do was visit the High Sierra where there is a region dedicated to his theory and where his memory prevails: the Evolution Range above Evolution Valley.

This is a weekend book about a weekend trip. I write it out of a classroom obligation to be Greek and Christian, to help students be reasonable, rational, and honest about their faith in an age when universities have a powerful role in defining what is reasonable. I write with the hope that students will, in various ways, learn that the academic life is a journey and not a destination, that academic disciplines are divergent paths not all leading to one place, and that, in universities, it is reasonable to believe the history of Jesus along with the natural history proposed by Charles Darwin.

2

Road Trip

The top of Mount Darwin is 13,831 feet above sea level at 37°10.02′N, 118°40.22′W. Getting to Mount Darwin from my small college in San Diego requires a six-hour drive veering slightly west of straight north. At the town of Bishop, the route turns southwest climbing to Lake Sabrina (elevation 9,128' and pronounced by the locals: sabr-eye-na). The hike from Sabrina to Mount Darwin is a little over ten miles. A three-day weekend offers enough time for the excursion.

Six of us were to go up Mount Darwin, but then the Anaheim Angels won the American League playoffs. The first two games of the World Series would be on the Saturday and Sunday of our trip. My two students from Orange County dropped out. So we were four: two history teachers, forty-four and thirty-one years old, and two boys, thirteen and ten years old. The boys, Matthew and Steven, are mine. David Nieman, the fourth, teaches high school history at Santa Fe Christian School in San Diego.

Our excursion party left at nine, lunched at Astro Burger in the High Desert, and got to the ranger station in Bishop a little after three. By 4:30 PM we were at Lake Sabrina. Matt and Steve sat in the far back of the station wagon facing backwards. They read books and passed CDs up to the front for the stereo. Dave and I talked. The temperature was in the low seventies for most of the trip, and since the car's air conditioner did not work, we drove with windows down. Few things are more fun than speeding down a two-lane desert highway, elbow in the breeze, backpacks loaded on top, mountains off in the distance. Having a window down—combined with the drone of the diesel engine—meant that conversation could not be dignified. Dave and I bantered back and forth mostly about teaching ancient world history and our methods for handling wild questions from our students about popular mysteries. Dave, after a minute of looking off to the row of huge signal dishes operated by the Owens Valley

Radio Observatory, turned back toward me, yelling: "So! What do you think of UFOs?"

There is serious academic work on UFOs by scientists, psychologists, and historians.[1] Any report of past events is grist for a historian's mill. Part of our job is handling the wild stories that get reported. The classroom goal in such cases is not so much a conclusion about what did or did not happen; rather, the goal is methodical and consistent thinking about reports of wild happenings. Historians working within the longest traditions of their academic discipline have an obligation to be open-minded, hear the evidence, take into account context, apply scales of reliability, and come to tentative conclusions that are socially acceptable. Being reasonable about history is always negotiated. The goal is a "best explanation" or set of "best explanations"—with "best" being a general agreement among respectable people.

Dave and I discussed the evidence for UFOs flown, presumably, by extraterrestrial life forms, that we have heard about from TV shows, grocery store magazines, and a few books. The problem is not a lack of evidence. The problem is in methodical and consistent thinking about the evidence.

David M. Jacobs is a model historian on the subject. He teaches at Temple University and wrote *Secret Life: Firsthand Accounts of UFO Abductions* (1992). In the first chapter, he explains his method of inquiry and argues for the academic reasonableness of his conclusions. He gathered a large number of abduction accounts and analyzed the diverse testimonies for consistencies. He then assessed the character and bias of the testifiers. Consistent with the Aristotelian-humanist tradition, he advocates that readers should not dismiss hard-to-believe testimony of abductions without first seriously looking into the character and circumstances of the testifiers. The most dubious aspect of his method is that he uses hypnotism to get into the subconscious of the testifiers. He justifies using hypnotism by noting it is increasingly used in jurisprudence and other academic fields such as psychology. (The book is endorsed by a professor of psychology at Harvard University.) After making a case for the reasonableness of his methods and the reliability of his sources, he sticks his neck out to say that the evidence warrants belief that alien abductions are occurring.

---

1. See also Sagan and Page, *UFO's: A Scientific Debate*.

Frankly, I don't think his case is persuasive or even offers a probable account for the evidence. Deep in the argument is the speculation that the aliens want to keep their presence secret, thus justifying the need for the researcher to use hypnotism to get the needed evidence. I am willing to believe a lot of weird things. I think history is wilder than is presented in textbooks. However, I draw the line at secret conspiracies where the lack of evidence is evidence. We have a hard enough time getting at what people want to flat-out tell us. If an alien conspiracy of silence requires the use of hypnotism to be revealed, I am not convinced. On the other hand, I liked the book, learned a lot, and appreciated the methodical inquiry. Books like his make it exciting to be a historian.

Dave and I teach world history to people who often have wide-angle openness to information, theories, and assertions. We ourselves want to be such people. We want to encourage such openness. But we also have a duty to teach students to think in well-disciplined, methodical ways.

The story of Noah's flood comes up in our history classes because it is the wildest reported event of natural history that comes down to us as an ancient oral tradition eventually written down in our ancient written sources. Along with the Genesis account of Noah's flood, we have an account with striking similarities found in *The Epic of Gilgamesh* that, like the Bible, is the story written from the perspective of a survivor saved by divine mercy. Natural historians have long sought confirmation in geology for the written reports. In the seventeenth and eighteenth centuries some of the most important natural philosophers of Europe worked to harmonize the Bible's story with what was known by geology, astronomy, and archeology.[2] Scientists today at the Institute for Creation Research in San Diego still work to find connections between natural history and the ancient accounts. The trouble with the project is that it is harder to do than it should be. Explaining the event is one thing; explaining why the event is not more geologically evident is even harder.

We Christians believe the Holy Spirit played a role in the writing and compilation of the Bible, but we have never agreed on the intent of the Holy Spirit in all the parts of the texts. Much of the Bible is intentional history, but much isn't. History, myth, and legend sometimes mix fact and metaphor to tell us things that are not exactly meant to be taken as reli-

2. See Cohn, *Noah's Flood*.

able reporting of events. Noah's flood, the dialogs of Job, and the book of Esther all point in historical directions, but may not be meant for the teaching of actual history.

The most interesting historian who inquired into the historical Noah is John Warwick Montgomery, who published *The Quest for Noah's Ark; a treasury of documented accounts from ancient times to the present day of sightings of the ark & explorations of Mount Ararat with a narration of the author's successful ascent to the summit of Noah's mountain* (1972). Montgomery gathered all the written and oral testimony available with the archeological goal of finding a piece of Noah's ark high in the Caucasus Mountains. He gathered together local oral traditions, narratives of earlier exploration, and possible sightings such as a 1916 speculative report by a Russian pilot. Most of the work for Montgomery, as always for historians, was in dusty archives. Making this all the more exciting, Montgomery was working during the Cold War in the borderlands with the former USSR.

Montgomery is a spark plug of a scholar. I met him at a conference of Christian historians in 1996. *The Quest for Noah's Ark* is a good book by an adventurous historian. That he is searching for something stuffy professors might laugh at makes the book all the more edgy. The problems he faces only get more complex as he digs deeper. He struggles with getting evidence, frustrated about the weakness of so much of it. He wrestles with all sorts of problems—even that we are not sure which mountain is the traditional Mount Ararat. Leaving the libraries, he picks one of the mountains, dons his climbing boots and trudges up into the ice to see if he can, himself, find the ark. Even better: he takes his son along with him for the trek, and the investigation becomes a family adventure.

That the book concludes with the ark unfound and the evidence still weak makes it all the more an example of a conscientious scholarly project. The academic world is better off because Montgomery has clarified some issues, organized and analyzed some evidence, done his best, and left it up to the next inquirer to take the adventure a step further. Montgomery himself believes that remnants of the ark are probably somewhere up high in the mountains because of his trust in the authority of the Genesis account; however, his religious commitments do not make him play false with his evidence or conclusion.

Montgomery and I were presenting papers in 1996 on the academic handling of reports of miracles. I felt honored to sit next to him. When I was a freshman in college I read his book *History and Christianity* (1965), which emphasizes the academic historian's role in affirming Jesus' resurrection. He obviously feels called as a historian to justify Christian history to the professional academic guild. To do so requires reminding the historical profession of its tradition of open-minded listening and inquiry into wild stories.

With my elbow in the breeze and a long, straight, high desert highway ahead, Dave and I were free to think about all sorts of historical issues. The classrooms we work in are also places where freedom rings. If it is reported to have happened in the past, then it is fair game for historical investigation. There are few things more enjoyable than a serious academic discussion in which students and faculty lose themselves in strategies pursuing understanding. The discussion is not free in the sense that anything said is equally valid; rather, the discussion is free because all reasonable options are assessed for their weaknesses and strengths. Much of any academic inquiry will move quickly into the realm of speculations based on assumptions. Such flights are to be expected. The work is in assessing the persuasiveness of these flights, pursuing the award of "best explanation available," and always humbly recognizing what we don't know. The university is at its best when it encourages such freedom. It is at its worst when it tries to restrict reasonable methods and conclusions.

I claim the freedom of my reasonableness. I also extend that same freedom to Darwin. I find Darwin to be a reasonable scientist whose methods and evidence support his speculations. It would be fun to have Darwin in the back seat with his elbow in the breeze. I hope that as we climb his mountain we will be able to feel close to him. He enjoyed climbing mountains in South America during his years on the *Beagle*. Like many of his class, he enjoyed rambling through the Alps on vacations.

Mount Darwin was named thirteen years after Charles Darwin (1809–1882) died. Darwin was born into a family that had little devotion to traditional Christianity. Both his grandfathers were famous for progressive thinking in science, industry, and theology. After graduating from college, Darwin found himself stuck in a career path leading toward the church because it was respectable. Darwin escaped entrapment in a church career to which he had no calling. He found, instead, adventure as a naturalist and captain's dinner companion on a five-year, round-the-world cruise from 1831 to 1836. Evident throughout his *Voyage of the Beagle* is a serious young man, diligent and humble. Also evident is a young man with very little interest in God. The Christian church appears in the book as an oppressor of Indians, and his accounts of camping and climbing adventures don't include outbursts of praise for the creator. On climbing a Chilean mountain he wrote, "Everyone must know the feeling of triumph and pride which a grand view from a height communicates to the mind." A little later he wrote of camping out: "The night was cloudless; and while lying in our beds, we enjoyed the sight (and it is a high enjoyment) of the multitude of stars which illumined the darkness of the forest."[3] He loved the mountains, the stars, and the forests, but never showed in his writings a love for God.

Coming from a family of no great Christian piety or biblical rootedness, Darwin easily slipped into vagueness about God and allowed his science increasingly to define his religion. Rich enough not to have a paying job, Darwin devoted himself to rigorous study of orchids, barnacles, worms, and all sorts of living things even though he was chronically ill. His diligence was rewarded by a rising reputation, but neither his illness, nor professional success, nor the deaths of beloved children brought him closer to God. His science seems to have simply encouraged his antagonism to traditional Christianity. Adrian Desmond and James Moore describe him in his later life as "an old Unitarian who had fallen off the feather bed. He was holding to a semi-respectable theism and packaging it under a designer label. . . . But his God was an absentee landlord, and nature self-sufficient."[4]

Darwin was a genteel, retiring man who loved the outdoors. He was a good man over whom the Bible's accounts of Jesus had no hold. His greatest achievement was a description of a theoretical mechanism of species creation that had no apparent need for a designer. If there was a God involved in the evolutionary process, Darwin wrote in *On the Origin of Species*, then it was "presumptuous" to think that God acted in the way taught by the churches.[5] Darwin himself began the academic tradition that evolution demands a new understanding of Christianity.

3. Darwin, *Voyage of the Beagle*, 298, 311.
4. Desmond and Moore, *Darwin*, 479.
5. Darwin, *Origin of the Species*, 188–89.

Darwin's book became the catalyst for new ways of thinking about God. Some Darwinians want to get rid of God altogether. Some want to keep a spiritualized creation without an active or communicating God. Some just want an intellectually respectable theism in which God is kept vague and distant. Kenneth Miller, a cell biologist at Brown University, has written a good book called *Finding Darwin's God: A Scientist's Search for Common Ground between God and Evolution* (1999). Miller declares his Christianity and his love of university research and appreciation of science. But the God in his title is too vague. Early in the book he defines God by the "great Western monotheistic traditions" and further distinguishes God for "truth, love, and knowledge."[6] But that definition and those characteristics don't fit traditional Christianity. Still, Miller is more traditionally Christian than Intelligent Design, a lawyerly movement that studiously avoids defining God by anything other than intelligence.

Christianity, if it is to be defined by its biblical foundation, has to be rooted in a relational God, immune to being abstracted, who came to earth as a human who suffered, died, and bodily rose as part of a plan of salvation. The tensions between Christianity and Darwinism can't be clarified by adopting an abstract, generic, creator God. Christians give away the store if they start that way. I have read too many books supposedly about Christianity and science that make no reference to the Bible and no mention of Jesus. Can a book really be about Christianity with no reference to the Bible and no mention of Jesus? A robust dialog between Christianity and Darwinism has to have the Christians standing on traditional foundations, not some vague, cookie-cutter monotheism. Christians believe in a God who became a man, was reported to have walked on water, redirected the weather, killed a tree, and made himself a nuisance to the laws of nature.

The peaks of the Evolution Group—Mount Darwin, Mount Haeckel, Mount Wallace, Mount Fiske, Mount Huxley, and Mount Spencer—were named by a twenty-five-year-old aspiring writer and member of the Sierra Club named Theodore Solomons (1870–1947). In 1895 he named a valley and contiguous basin "Evolution," and the major peaks bounding the east side of the valley and basin after those whom he called "the great evolu-

---

6. Miller, *Finding Darwin's God*, 267.

tionists."[7] The names he chose to attach to mountains were not just those of famous scientists; rather, he chose the names of promoters of evolution, especially promoters of the spiritual implications of evolution. Solomons' mother was a theosophist—a believer in vital spiritual truths communicated in the wisdom of many ancient religions. She taught her son to be skeptical of modern, organized, institutionalized religions. His sister became a theosophist and astrologer. Solomons liked the way Darwin's evolution had opened the way to thinking about spiritual influences in natural history. He named the mountains of the Evolution Range after personal heroes. Wallace was the most prominent scientist in the world doing systematic observations of séances and other communications with spirits. Fiske was the Darwinist who was probably closest to Solomons' personal model. A famous writer and lecturer, Fiske promoted modern thought while debunking Christianity.

Hiking into the Evolution Range of the Sierra Nevada is for me as much about young Solomons' mind and goals as it is about Darwin's methods of natural history. Solomons turned this region of the High Sierra into a cartographical monument to religious progress as much as scientific progress. I come to these mountains as a traditionalist wary of progress. But I am not an antagonist. I can appreciate what young Solomons was doing.

Of the people Solomons awarded a mountain, the two I am least sympathetic to are Huxley and Spencer. Thomas Henry Huxley (1825–1895) died the summer Solomons named a mountain after him. He was "Darwin's bulldog" and is, to me, the least appealing of the "great evolutionists." He was the kind of one-sided person who clamps onto an idea and won't moderate in any way. Paradoxes, conundrums, uncertainties, and a humble furrowing of the brow were not his cup of tea. He was in his glory when in debate—the art of pushing an opponent into a corner—and he often targeted Christians. He coined the term "agnosticism," unwillingness to commit oneself to doctrines about God, but he did so as a debating ploy rather than in a spirit of true humility. There is a long tra-

---

7. Solomons, "Beginnings of the John Muir Trail," 34. After finishing his 1895 survey, he wrote articles on his work in *The Sierra Club Bulletin*, *The Traveller*, *The Overland Monthly*, and *Appalachia: The Journal of the Appalachian Mountain Club*. These articles helped popularize the names Solomons bestowed on natural features. The names were also supported by Sierra Club members who further surveyed the trail, most importantly Walter A. Starr and Joseph N. LeConte. Solomons himself soon left California for Alaska, then New York. See the obituary by Farquhar in *Sierra Club Bulletin* 33, no. 3:117-18. The only full biography is Sargent's, *Solomons of the Sierra*.

dition in Western philosophy going back to Pyhrro of Elis (c.360–270 BC) of humble doubt coupled with refusal to affirm one position or another. Many agnostics conscientiously struggle with belief in the resurrection. Huxley, however, was an evangelist for Darwinism using agnosticism in religion as a means to undermine his enemies.

Huxley liked things simple. As a member of the London School Board, Huxley was against the traditional curriculum's diversity. He wanted schools to teach science as a progressive and single-minded truth system. "As our race approaches its maturity," he wrote, "it discovers, as I believe it will, that there is but one kind of knowledge and but one method of acquiring it."[8]

Herbert Spencer (1820–1903) was, like Huxley, a grand unifier of all things physical, social, and intellectual under the umbrella of Darwinian evolution. Spencer saw a profound simplicity in Darwin's theory that could be applied widely, even into the social sciences, especially sociology. Spencer coined the term Social Darwinism. Richard Hofstadter in *Social Darwinism in American Thought* noted that Spencer became fashionable among intellectuals because he promoted a Darwinism "large enough to be all things to all men."[9]

Solomons apparently appreciated this style of over-hyped Darwinism, but unlike Huxley and Spencer, Solomons was intensely interested in the interaction between material and spiritual nature. Solomons' choices for other mountain names were men who promoted progressive religion founded on facts from the natural sciences.

Probably the most famous Darwinian of Solomons' era was Ernst Haeckel (1834–1919). Unlike Huxley, Haeckel wanted nothing to do with debating ploys. He had all the fire of Huxley but added the endearing quality of not being a calculating orator or narrow thinker. He had big ideas full of his own version of intellectual hope. Haeckel was Germany's most famous Darwinist when Solomons named a mountain after him in 1895. As professor of zoology at the University of Jena, he had become famous for creating his own theory of everything: *Monism*. He taught that old traditions of God as creator needed to be swept aside. "Anthropism," he preached, needed to be destroyed. Anthropism was the "powerful and world-wide group of erroneous opinions" that assert that humans are spe-

---

8. Huxley, "Advisableness," 21.
9. Hofstadter, *Social Darwinism*, 24, 31.

cially created with a special purpose.¹⁰ Like many scientists, he merged his scientific research with a professorial sense of responsibility to teach what he believed to be the philosophic and religious implications of his research. He believed that by "courageous effort to attain the truth, and by a clear view of the world" scientists can persuade people to give up the superstitions of traditional Christianity and embrace his truth that the cosmos is eternal and infinite and made up of matter and energy. "Eternal motion runs through infinite time in an unbroken development."¹¹

Solomons, a young man of the Sierra Club, was much taken with Haeckel's courage and intellect. It was Haeckel who invented the term *ecology*. Haeckel's monism assumed a type of psychic energy at work in cosmic evolution. He apparently was encouraged in this by the early work of Jean Baptiste Lamarck (1744–1829). Haeckel believed Lamarck's ideas were the foundation upon which Darwin developed the theory of evolution. Darwin himself said no such thing and often criticized Lamarck. Solomons did not name Mount Lamarck, but the name fits the interwoven science and spiritualism of the area.

By naming the mountain just south of Haeckel after Alfred Russel Wallace (1823–1913), Solomons was honoring an evolutionist well known for his attempts in England and America to promote the evidence for communication with dead people. Wallace had lectured in San Francisco in 1887, and it is possible that Solomons had attended the lectures as a teenager. Wallace wanted nothing to do with traditional Christianity, yet he thought natural selection could not account for the human mind and the communications with spirits that he experienced in séances. Wallace comes down to us in history as outdoing even Darwin as a gentle and dedicated gatherer of observational evidence. His gentleness is best known in his willingness to let Darwin preempt his announcement of his own theory of natural selection. Wallace came up with the theory in 1857 while fighting a fever in Malaysia. He quickly dashed it off in the mail to Charles Lyell (1797–1875), who has the highest peak in Yosemite National Park named after him. Lyell alerted Darwin and eventually a deal was struck that Darwin's and Wallace's papers would be read together at the Linnean Society on July 1, 1858. Wallace had generated his theories independently, but he always told people that Darwin deserved the greater

---

10. Haeckel, *Riddle of the Universe*, 11.
11. Ibid., 13.

credit. Wallace wrote of Darwin: "His name should, in my opinion, stand above that of every other philosopher of ancient or modern times. The force of admiration can no further go!!!"[12]

But Wallace did not think his and Darwin's theory of natural selection could account for the human mind and was suspicious of putting too much emphasis on mere sexual selection. He was convinced of the existence of a spiritual world and a spiritual nature in humans. He lectured widely on the human mind, communication with the spiritual world, life after death, and miracles. Wallace made his living and his fame by being a keen observer, and no amount of giggling or scoffing could make him deny that he had observed and experienced spiritual activity. In 1887 Wallace lectured in San Francisco, met John Muir, and visited the Calaveras grove of giant sequoias on the western slope of the Sierra Nevada. "Of all the natural wonders he saw in America," notes his biographer, "nothing impressed him so much as these glorious trees."[13]

Theodore Solomons, deep in one of the most isolated areas of the Sierra Nevada and apparently moved by the power of Darwinism to bring new understanding to everything, named the peaks overlooking his Evolution Valley not after the most famous geologists of the world; rather, he named them after the most famous proponents of how Darwinism should change humanity's way of thinking about religion. Religion could never be the same after Darwin. Huxley attacked tradition. Haeckel advocated a universal, non-personal, psychic force at work in the cosmos. Wallace had become a stump speaker for spiritualism. Spencer promoted a social Darwinism. And although Spencer avoided religious matters in his writings, John Fiske promoted what he thought was Spencer's religious version of social Darwinism.

John Fiske (1842–1901), another non-scientist, may be the key to understanding all Solomons' choices. It is easy to imagine that when Solomons was sitting on the valley floor naming the peaks he had in his knapsack a copy of Fiske's collection of essays, *Excursions of an Evolutionist* (1883). It makes perfect sense—though there is no evidence, just pure speculation—that Solomons was reading Fiske when he looked up and named the peaks. *Excursions of an Evolutionist* not only includes Fiske's praise of Spencer as one whose work is of the caliber of Aristotle

---

12. Raby, *Alfred Russell Wallace*, 151.
13. Ibid., 245.

and Newton, but also has a long essay, "*In Memoriam:* Charles Darwin," written on the day of Darwin's burial in 1882 as a "tribute to the memory of the beautiful and glorious life that has just passed away from us."[14]

John Fiske was in college at Harvard when he discovered the expansive power of evolution in a book by Spencer. He wrote home to his mother that Spencer "has discovered a great law of evolution in nature, which underlies all phenomena & which is as important & more comprehensive than Newton's law of gravitation."[15] Unable to gain an academic post in Harvard's history department, Fiske first became a librarian and then a popular writer and traveling speaker. There is a good chance Solomons heard Fiske speak in San Francisco in 1892, just three years before naming a mountain in honor of him. Fiske wrote that he met John Muir at that time.[16] Fiske was most famous for the two-volume *Outlines of Cosmic Philosophy* (1874), in which he stretched Spencer's evolutionary ideas into religion in ways similar to Haeckel's monism. In his memorial essay, Fiske insisted that "Mr. Darwin's work" has been "to remodel the theological conceptions of the origin and destiny of man."[17] Conceptions of God and religion, for Fiske, had been reformed root and branch because of Darwin:

> No religious creed that man has ever devised can be made to harmonize in all its features with modern knowledge. All such creeds were constructed with reference of theories of the universe which are now utterly and hopelessly discredited. . . . Is not the belief in God perhaps a dream of the childhood of our race, like the belief in elves and bogarts which once were no less universal? and is not modern science fast destroying the one as it has already destroyed the other?[18]

If I understand Solomons right, when he said he named the mountains after "the great evolutionists," he was not really thinking much about science. He was not a scientist; he was an aspiring writer and progressive from a theosophist family. He was thinking about religion, the cosmos, what Douglas Adams called "Life, the Universe, and Everything."

---

14. Fiske, *Excursions*, 22.
15. Quoted in *Dictionary of National Biography*, s.v. "Fiske, John."
16. Winston, *John Fiske*, 107.
17. Fiske, *Excursions*, 368.
18. Quoted in Winston, *John Fiske*, 81–82.

Solomons was thinking the grandest thoughts possible as he mapped one of the grandest valleys and mountain ranges in America. His mind turned to the people who aspired to put behind them the old religion and propose new religious interpretations of the cosmos. I think it was Fiske that he had in his knapsack. In one of the essays on Spencer and sociology in *Excursions of an Evolutionist*, Fiske praises "the truly philosophic character of Mr. Darwin's method."[19] This is the spirit honored in Solomons' Evolution Range of peaks. He was not honoring scientists as scientists; rather, scientists as philosophers, as professors, as religious reformers.

There are two other people who names on maps of the region enhance the scientific, philosophic, and religious aura of the Evolution Range. Both were founders of the Sierra Club: Joseph LeConte (1823–1901) and John Muir (1838–1914). LeConte led the first group of university students into the Sierra in the summer of 1870. In the fall of 1869, he and his brother John had enrolled the first students into the new land-grant university in Oakland. A story is told that Joseph handed a pen to enroll a young man, saying, "You have the honor to be the first student to register in this institution that is destined to be one of the very greatest in the country."[20] Joseph was the first geology professor in what did become one of the world's great universities: the University of California at Berkeley. He and his son both eventually got peaks named after them, and both did a fair amount of naming mountains themselves. At the end of that first academic year, eight students invited LeConte to join them on a geologizing ramble in the Sierra Nevada. He called the group the "University Excursion Party" and published an account of the trip. LeConte's *A Journal of Ramblings Through the High Sierras of California by the "University Excursion Party"* (1875) begins with the party saddling their horses in Oakland on July 27 and heading east. The journal is most famous for its August 5 entry:

> To-day to Yosemite Falls. This has been the hardest day's experience yet. We thought we had plenty of time, and therefore started late. Stopped a moment at the foot of the Falls, at a saw-mill, to make inquires. Here found a man in rough miller's garb, whose intelligent face and earnest, clear blue eye, excited my interest. After

---

19. Fiske, *Excursions*, 175.

20. Shenk, "Introduction," to LeConte, *Journal*, viii. This story is not attributed to a source and does not appear in LeConte's autobiography.

some conversation, discovered that it was Mr. Muir, a gentleman of whom I had heard much about.... We were glad to meet each other. I urged him to go with us to Mono, and he seemed disposed to do so.[21]

It is hard not to like Joseph LeConte. Muir remembered the day in Yosemite Valley when he met LeConte and his students: "I gladly left all my other work and followed him. This first LeConte excursion, with its grand landscapes and weather and delightful campfire talks, though now far back in the days of auld lang syne, still remains in mind bright and indestructible, like glacial inscriptions on granite."[22]

LeConte was a soft-spoken man who believed that Darwin's discoveries and theory of a completely natural mechanism that could account for the creation of diverse species required every person who aspired to be intellectually respectable to reorient their understanding of religion. He did not want to press the issue. He was not bombastic. He was confident that a religious reorientation would evolve slowly as society progressed. Two years after Solomons named the peaks of the Evolution Range, LeConte published a set of public lectures called *Evolution and Its Relation to Religious Thought* (1897). LeConte was sure that the theory of evolution would soon be incorporated into the Christian mind in the same way that the sun-centered view of Copernicus was eventually accepted by Christians. What LeConte could not abide was the notion that Darwinism would be used to undermine God's active role in creation. "God," LeConte wrote in 1884, "is ever present and ever working in nature."[23] LeConte believed that truth would prevail and that science and Christianity would not be found contradictory in the long run. Christianity and Darwinism,

---

21. LeConte, *Journal*, 41. Solomons in 1895 was surveying what would become the John Muir Trail when he named the Evolution Group. The John Muir Trail runs south from Yosemite Valley through Evolution Valley to Mount Whitney over 212 miles in the most rugged region of the High Sierra. Muir Pass is 11,955 feet and separates Evolution Basin from LeConte Canyon—named for Joseph's son, Joseph Nisbet LeConte who, as a new graduate of UC Berkeley in 1890, spent the summer packing through the High Sierra with some school buddies. In 1908, "Little Joe" LeConte and two friends from the Sierra Club attempted to be the first to pack their way through the trail Solomons had begun a decade before. Muir died in December of 1914 and the state legislature named the trail in 1915 at the request of Sierra Club.

22. LeConte, *Journal*, 109.

23. Stephens, *Joseph LeConte*, 169. Matthew S. Abajian, in a student paper, alerted me to this passage.

rightly understood, were compatible and eventually people would wonder what the fuss was about.

The trouble with LeConte was that both his Christianity and his Darwinism were a bit vague. In his autobiography, LeConte wrote that he tithed to all the churches in his neighborhood without regularly attending any of them. "So far as churches are concerned," he wrote, "I could never take a very active part in any, because it seemed to me that they were all too narrow in their views."[24] When attacked by a local minister for leading the young astray with his classes on evolution, LeConte did not reply. The university newspaper, *The Berkeleyan*, defended him, declaring that "the attacks on the teachings of our beloved Professor LeConte by certain barbarians in the world of thought, deserve no more than a passing reference."[25]

At forty-five, LeConte had come to San Francisco to find personal peace and hope after the rancor of teaching in South Carolina and Georgia in the years surrounding the Civil War. Temperamentally unsuited to controversy, he returned every summer to the Sierra Nevada with his students and his friends in the Sierra Club. During the last decades of his life, he published more than ever before and found California to be his land of peace and plenty. From 1903 to 1904, the Sierra Club erected a chapel-like memorial lodge dedicated to LeConte in Yosemite Valley. Between John Muir, the exuberant controversialist, and LeConte, the optimistic quietist, the Sierra Club had their two founding saints. Both scientific and both spiritual, they exemplify the way evolution and Christianity can be one when neither the science nor the religion is taken too seriously. Here is a typical quote from LeConte's *Evolution, Its Nature, Its Evidences, and Its Relation to Religious Thought* (1897):

> Infinite space and the universal law of gravitation; infinite time and the universal law of evolution. These two are the grandest ideas in the realm of thought. The one is universal sustentation, the other universal creation, by law. There is one law and one energy pervading all space stretching through all time. Our religious philosophy has long ago accepted the one, but has not yet had time to readjust itself completely to the other.[26]

---

24. LeConte, *Autobiography*, 265.
25. Stephens, *Joseph LeConte*, 183.
26. LeConte, *Evolution*, 282–83.

Road Trip

Around the campfire, LeConte, Muir, and the Berkeley students could wax eloquent about infinite time and the universal law of evolution that created the mountains they camped beneath. I am not so romantic. As much as I would love to share a campfire with LeConte and Muir, I am distrustful of scientific claims to universality—let alone appeals to infinite time. I think being reasonable about science and religion is more complicated and certainly requires a greater sense of the limits of what we know and how we know.

Christianity is not supposed to be romantic. Christianity is prosaic. Darwinists can wax eloquent about near-infinite time, universal laws, and the ultimate beauty of development, for Darwinism is a big theory about long history. But biblical Christianity is irritating and unpleasant. Abraham is a cowardly liar. David is a murderous adulterer, leader of a severely dysfunctional family. Most of the main characters we meet in the Old and New Testaments would be hard to work with. Laws and judgments are unstable in the Bible. God relents to negotiations. Jesus seems to recommend whiny petitioning that will wear God down. The whole story of the Bible pulls together as a history of undeserved salvation. As for nature, even though the Psalms wax eloquent about creation, apparently the whole thing is going to be rolled up in the end. Some form of new creation is indicated for the future. As for people, many bystanders die horrible deaths. Children are killed. Children suffer.

History is not a romantic discipline. Historians in general are best at causing intellectual problems, not solving them. We find the flaws in heroes and the problems with grand public policies. Historians rarely find or preach the simplicity of it all. Ours is one of the few academic disciplines that do not believe that the simplest answers are probably the truest. We thrive in complexity, disorder, and the general messiness of human life.

What could be less romantic than a Christian historian?

The ranger station in the town of Bishop is a multi-gabled Western ranch house. Inside, Dave, the boys, and I stood in line waiting for the young woman ranger to give us a wilderness permit and tell us the trail regulations. I asked the ranger about the boys being able to climb Mount Darwin. She said it would be a push but was pleasant and smiled at the kids.

Leaving Bishop, the road to Lake Sabrina climbed fast while the temperature dropped. It is a minor matter of joy to me that, upon arriving at a campsite near Lake Sabrina, I can now, as a father, get out of the car and say, "Boys, you set up the tent and lay your sleeping bags out while I go look around." This of course does not mean that they won't be goofing around by the creek with no tent in sight when I come back; however, there is joy in the idea that the kids can carry some of the weight of the trip.

After dinner, the temperature was in the 30s on its way to the 20s. The boys and I went to bed early to keep warm. Three of us in a two-man tent was cozy. Around midnight I got up. The sky was crisp with sparkling stars. Standing out on a rock at high altitude looking into a clear night sky, I sensed the complexity of time. What I see with my eyes are reports from millions of separate instances ranging over millions of years. Multiple times are registering at what is to me present time. "Nothing puzzles me more than time and space; and yet nothing troubles me less."[27] I know nothing of the quote's context, but shouldn't I be troubled by what I was looking at?

Time is a wonder. It is not a line. It is not a circle. Time and distances shrink with acceleration and lengthen with deceleration. Speed, not time, is a constant in Albert Einstein's theory of relativity. Time is something wholly different than any analogy we use to try to describe it. The Bible pictures past, present, and future as entwined with Jesus at the fullness. Time isn't a line. It is like a cup overflowing. It lays back on itself like bread being kneaded. John the Baptist declares that the one who comes after him was before him.[28] Maybe the sun standing still for Joshua was actually God speeding up the time surrounding Joshua.

Astronomers are awash in the wildness of time. Like historians, astronomers try to domesticate time, to make it into a manageable model, but time refuses to be made easy. Historians and astronomers like to think of themselves as standing on a dock studying the sea, when really there is no dock and everybody is swimming in that sea without a lifejacket.

Physics tells us that light is squirrelly. It can be bent or even sucked into darkness by gravity. The speed of light is a boundary in physics; but, then again, it doesn't work all the time like a boundary. As a believer in

27. Burnham, et. al., *Guide to Backyard Astronomy*, 13.
28. John 1:15.

miracles, I take comfort in reading books by mathematicians and physicists who wonder at the apparent lack of physical or mathematical logic in some of the things we experimentally see that defy common sense.

Time is squirrelly. Roger Penrose, a mathematician willing to contemplate the puzzlements of physical reality, describes the possibility of a *causality violation* in which a signal can be sent from a future event to cause a past event.[29] Of course, the math doesn't justify movies like *Back to the Future* or the *Star Trek* episodes I enjoyed as a kid; however, reading about the amazing possibilities in physics makes it easier for me to read accounts of miracles. The more we know about God from the Bible and about God's creation from the mathematicians and physicists, the less anyone should think that God or nature is known best by formal logic. Certainly logic gets all of us pretty far toward understanding; but logic does not satisfy. Time, space, the very small, and the very fast make crooked the straight ways of logic and common sense. The preacher asks: "Who can straighten what God has made crooked?"[30]

There are Christian astronomers trying to work with alternative physics and astronomy to support their assertion that the universe is much younger than supposed.[31] Hugh Ross is a Christian astronomer who finds much in normal academic astronomy to support the Bible's story of creation. Maybe they are on the right track. I don't know. As for me, I look up at the night sky and wonder.

Carl Sagan (1934–1996) was a professor of astrophysics at Cornell University who became a pop icon of the 70s and 80s with his television series *Cosmos*, his novel (now movie) *Contact*, and his government-funded project to listen for messages from space called SETI (Search for Extra Terrestrial Intelligence). Johnny Carson on late night television had a comedy routine imitating Sagan's way of trying to impress people that there were "billions and billions of stars." To his own huge audiences, Sagan taught that humans should be humbled by the size and age of the universe. Part of his belief that there might be intelligent life on other planets came from a humble insistence that humans should not think themselves too special. If people wanted to feel special, they could remember that they

---

29. Penrose, *Road to Reality*, 401–10.
30. Eccl 7:13.
31. For a young-earth astronomer's views, see DeYoung, *Astronomy and Creation*, and a less technical book for college students, *Astronomy and the Bible*.

are partly made of atoms that were born in stars that exploded long ago. "We are made of star-stuff," he would say.[32]

I stood out in the cold for a while looking at the sky. I felt humbled by the stars; however, what makes me special is not leftover atoms from stars. The God who created and sustains the universe loves me and communicates with me. Such thoughts are astonishingly cocky by all human standards. Christians are guilty of thinking themselves absurdly special in a vast cosmos. The God of it all wants to communicate with you and me.

William Dembski, in his book *Intelligent Design: The Bridge Between Science and Theology* (1999), points out that SETI shows that when scientists find patterns in nature—in this case some high level of patterned complexity in the radio waves that wash through the universe—they infer intelligence behind the pattern. Dembski further points out that most scientists change the rules of this game when any Christian scientist infers in a similar way the action of an Intelligent Designer. Dembski is right about the double standard; however, looking at the crisp stars, I am not much interested in an Intelligent Designer. Historians wrestle mostly with the individuality of people and human events. I am interested in the human speech and actions of Jesus.

Here in the mountains, away from my classroom, the stars don't inspire me with the natural order and mathematical simplicity of the cosmos. I don't worship an Intelligent Designer. I am overwhelmed by the disorders of time when I look into the night sky. "Nothing puzzles me more than time and space; and yet nothing troubles me less." I worry more about the overconfidence of academic disciplines than about the gullibility of people.

Do I sound jaded about scientific discovery? I don't feel jaded. It would be fun to have Carl Sagan standing with me on a rock looking at stars. He was humble enough to allow himself to promote what people laughed at: the search for extraterrestrial intelligence. He was cocky enough to become a television "personality" preaching the vastness of the cosmos and the lack of any God out there. He was smart and loved the information that his discipline produced. I could learn a lot from Sagan. I flatter myself that he would enjoy having a willing student like me sighting stars down his arm as he pointed into the sky.

---

32. McDonough, "Star Stuff," Skeptic, 10–17.

Road Trip

I have been blessed in life to work in university settings and further blessed to have had long conversations with very smart people. There are few things more fun than a bunch of faculty sitting around a dinner table. Get everybody away from grant-writing rhetoric, away from textbook simplicities, away from posturing for publication, away from professionalism, and into a friendly conversation about what we know, what we don't know, and the limitations of the ways we do investigations—then you have the makings of not only a great evening, but a great university.

3

Base Camp

The car gave us trouble in the morning. The parking area for the trailhead was a little over a mile away but up another thousand feet. My twenty-year-old diesel motor needed much coaxing to start and the transmission would not shift out of first gear. We chugged and faltered our way to a parking spot where I pointed the thing downhill and turned off the engine. The car doesn't lock, so we made it look locked, then headed up the road to the trailhead at Lake Sabrina.

Small groves of aspen trees were brilliantly golden, but most of the trees around us were Douglas fir. The redwoods on the coast are more romantic. The giant sequoia are more impressive, but they are only found in relatively small groves between 4,000 and 8,000 feet on the western slope of the Sierra. The oldest trees in the world, the bristlecone pine, are scraggly little things and can be found on the other side of the Owens Valley. The Douglas fir all around us were pushing a hundred feet tall, but something about these trees makes them neither romantic nor impressive.

The diversity of tree life is the kind of intellectual problem Darwin tried to solve. The problem was two-sided for Darwin. On the one hand, there seemed to be too much diversity for his conception of God as efficient creator. Would a God of good order have created the world with so much diversity? Darwin did not think so. On the other hand, there wasn't enough diversity if species simply multiplied randomly.[1] There must be a natural law or mechanism at work.

His book, *On the Origin of Species,* proposed a two-stage mechanism that creates and limits the diversity of species: first random variation, then natural selection. The power of the book was not that it compels assent by collecting lots of facts that prove its central tenets; rather, the book's power

---

1. Darwin, *Origin of Species*, 279–80.

is that it offers a mechanism in the system of nature that historically accounts for the not-too-much-but-not-too-little diversity of species.

The book has increased in influence since Darwin wrote it, but *not* because his speculative model has been fully tested. The existence of a mechanism wholly "random" and wholly "natural" cannot be completely observed or tested. The existence of a variation and selection mechanism in nature has been proven in some narrow laboratory circumstances, but the amazing confidence in Darwinian evolution as a biological "best explanation" comes from what might be called "time-testing." Darwin's speculation that a unseen two-stage mechanism was at work throughout history keeps working and even serves biologists better now than it did a hundred years ago. Even with the discovery of genetics, DNA, and the most recent molecular observations, Darwin's theory keeps offering the best explanation for what is happening. Darwin's mechanism has gained so much credibility that there are now university disciplines such as sociobiology that use evolution as the foundation for inquiry and explanation. Darwin's theory has legs. It has vast explanatory power. In many cases it even predicts what later will be discovered. Although there are big mysteries still out there, "black boxes" where Darwin's theory is seriously strained, Darwin's theory is one of the hardest working theories in science and continues to be more successful than not. Darwin's two-stage mechanism cannot be proven true in the strictest sense because it depends on unprovable assumptions of randomness and naturalness. Proof would also require a set of observations over huge lengths of time that are impossible. What we have are lots of observations in laboratory settings and fossil remains that point to the near absolute certainty that some means of variation and selection are happening in nature all around us. Being unprovable is not a deal breaker for a hard-working theory like Darwin's.

The sciences that make grand historical statements about natural events, such as cosmology, geology, astronomy, and evolutionary biology, are full of assumptions and speculations. Such sciences seek credibility and authority rather than proof. Credibility and authority goes to theories with incrementally accumulated corroborating evidence that serves increasingly to generate more confidence. When genetics was discovered, it fit perfectly with Darwin's theory.

The academic world is very practical. University research focuses on what works. Few professors live in ivory towers. All university disciplines are looking for explanations that work in the sense that members of the academic community can use them to connect to related theories or encourage the finding of new information. The "best explanations" do the most work. In the pragmatic world of academics, what works gains credibility and authority as truth.

This is one of the reasons I am on a trail headed into the Evolution Range. I know Darwin's theory works within the boundaries of credibility that are standard to natural history. I just don't think it is true to the extent that it should influence the core of Christian history. The Evolution Range of the Sierra Nevada honors many progressive men who embraced Darwinism as true to the extreme extent of then insisting that Christianity, therefore, could not be true—that some new version of spirituality or a new conception of God needed to be created to fit Darwinism. These university men insisted that reasonable people with the courage to be honest with the facts will see that Darwin removed humanity's need for a creator God who gives purpose to creation. Psalm 104 is good poetry but there is nothing factually true in lines such as:

> He makes grass grow for the cattle, and plants for man to cultivate. . . .
>
> The trees of the Lord are well watered, the cedars of Lebanon that he planted.

Trudging up to Mount Darwin, I think the grass and trees around me actually are given purpose by God. I believe he picked cedars for Lebanon and aspen for Lake Sabrina. But I also know that a mechanism of variation and selection is in the creative mix too. We are trudging into a wilderness designated on maps to honor people who would think me, at best, superstitious and, at worst, dishonest. I came here to be among them out of a sense of obligation as a Christian loyal to university life and thought. I want to be reasonable. I want to be honest with the facts. I need evidence in order to enter academic discussions. If my Christianity is to stand strong in universities, strong enough to stand unchanged beside Darwinian natural history, I need to remind myself as to the meaning and methods of being reasonable in a university.

The boys usually have a hiking game that they can play for hours. Someone says "I've got one"—meaning the name of a baseball player. Everybody gets to ask "yes" or "no" questions. The goal is to ask as few questions as possible before getting at the name. The method of winning entails identifying overlapping categories then isolating increasingly smaller subsets: retired > National League > West > California > outfielder > Is it Willie Mays? Detective novels and suspense movies often rely on this method. No special training is necessary. This method of inquiry is often used in various academic disciplines; however, the sciences and humanities have developed many, more sophisticated, methods of inquiry.

University professors use these methods to produce facts, ideas, and conclusions that are often in tension with each other and sometimes contradictory. At any one time, teachers and students have to hold on to knowledge that is impossible to unify. There are, however, many people in universities who are confident that all human knowledge will gather into a great unity someday. They believe that all true information points toward a highest, single, simple Truth that every honest thinker should recognize. I don't think this idea is supportable by evidence or biblical. God is Truth and gives humans some information; however, there is lots of true information created by humans that has yet to be reconciled. Physics, for example, is a university discipline that is learning about things that don't seem to be reconcilable into a single system. Political science is full of information that works here but not there. Logicians and mathematicians can create wholly separate though valid structures of thought based on distinct sets of axioms. I believe Paul when he says I will someday "know fully, even as I am fully known;" however, he was not talking about me knowing whether light is a particle or wave, whether republican separation of powers is the best policy for every nation, and whether Euclid was right or wrong about there being ten axioms.[2]

Darwinism's most adamant proponents have tended to insist that their discipline has produced a simple Truth to which any rational person must submit. Thomas Huxley, "Darwin's bulldog," harped about a unified simple rationality that *obviously* supported Darwin and not the Bible. Richard Dawkins, one of Darwin's modern bulldogs, praises the "Anglo-Saxon simplicity" that "all questions about life have the same answer (although it may not always be a helpful one): natural selection."[3]

One way to categorize college professors—an overgeneralization but a useful one for the purpose of understanding Huxley and Dawkins—is to

---

2. 1 Cor 13:12.
3. Dawkins, *Climbing Mount Improbable*, 228.

split them into *Totalizers* and *Tentative Investigators*. There are Darwinist and Christian professors of both types.

Totalizers use their classrooms to preach that if all people are perfectly rational they will all ultimately agree. Usually there is some sort of declaration that the progress of knowledge has one glorious end: light will be figured out, democracy will prove best for all, and natural selection will answer all questions about life. All rational people ride one train of progress together. *Tentative Investigators* are wimpy. Ask them a question and they give you at least two answers joined by "on the other hand." The *Totalizers* are the more popular teachers, their books are easier to read, and the news media finds them easier to interview. *Tentative Investigators* are like cats. They can't be herded and can rest easy in the midst of household chaos. *Tentative Investigators* don't disagree with the notion that knowledge is progressing; however, they are pretty sure that progress is uneven, experiencing fits and starts, and that we can never be sure at any one point whether we are taking one step backward or two steps forward. *Totalizers* are often scared that someone—especially some religious or political authority—is going to block progress. *Tentative Investigators* are less worried that progress can be stopped.

Richard Dawkins is a *Totalizer*. Among the Greeks, Plato was a *Totalizer*. Plato preached a triumphal, Dawkins-style, one-size-fits-all rationalism. Socrates, Plato's hero, in over a thousand pages of *Dialogues,* never finds himself to be wrong. Socrates is rational, smart, and tricky, and he never has to apologize. Plato and Socrates give the impression that rationality and smartness lead in one direction and tend toward consensus.

Me? I believe God is Truth, but I don't think we have any reason to think human reason is the best path to that Truth. Isaiah speaks the word of the Lord: "For my thoughts are not your thoughts, neither are your ways my ways."[4] I find truth in the wisdom of Saint Augustine, who saw all our activities and thoughts in this world as mixed up, screwed up, filled with God's communications and actions but clouded by the Devil's hold on humans and human institutions. I am a big believer in the practical value of being trained in reasoning skills and the responsibilities of rationality. Universities are the institutions where we pursue and teach the practice and responsibilities of reasoning. However, I am wary of professors promoting university classrooms as cars on the train to Truth. Universities

4. Isa 55:8.

are not churches. Professors are not priests. University classrooms are glorious spaces of information and inquiry, but they have no single purpose or destination. In my classrooms I try to promote the values of tentative investigation. We are looking for best explanations and viable traditions that may point to possible truths and maybe even to the Truth. Students should experience the confusions in intellectual life and then learn the skills of trying to make sense, plausible sense, maybe even persuasive sense, out of available information. I am not afraid to let my classroom ponder what the Truth might be, but I warn them that overconfidence is dangerous. My model in the classroom is not Socrates; it is Aristotle.

Aristotle (384–322 BC) is most often presented in textbooks as a systematic thinker who knew exactly what he was doing. However, if you read his books, you will realize that he was a *Tentative Investigator*, a tinkerer in multiple disciplines. Sometimes he played the philosopher in Plato's walled orchard, but he could also be found knee-deep in tide pools or dust-covered in historical studies. His books, which often appear to be more lecture notes than monographs, are a mishmash of insightful but often inconsistent strategies to get at whatever was on his mind at the time or whatever he was supposed to be teaching a student. He was willing to do the best he could with what he had before him. With this attitude, he became a founder of many disciplines such as logic, physics, biology, literary criticism, political science, history, and psychology.

Back when I was a student, I read two books that impressed me with the importance of Aristotle: *Zen and the Art of Motorcycle Maintenance* (1974), a travel-thinking book, and *Saint Thomas Aquinas: "The Dumb Ox"* by G. K. Chesterton. The tinkering, earthy, humanistic Aristotle is a theme in both. Over the decades since then I have increasingly understood why I love university life in Aristotelian terms. G. K. Chesterton wrote that Aristotelian thinking

> might be a humbler or homelier thing than the Platonic mind; that is why it was Christian. St. Thomas [Aquinas] was, if you will, taking the lower road when he walked in the steps of Aristotle. So was God, when He worked in the workshop of Joseph.[5]

---

5. Chesterton, *Saint Thomas Aquinas*, 42.

The line about Joseph's workshop is a Chestertonian flourish, but it is linked to the way Aristotle combined his various thinking strategies into one book titled *Organon,* a term that can be translated as "toolbox." For the purpose of a thoughtful mountain climb, the *Organon* might be best pictured as a pocketknife, the Swiss Army kind with multiple folding tools.

When studying plants and animals, Aristotle developed two strategies of categorizing. Depending on what the inquirer is interested in, he or she can categorize things vertically or horizontally. Vertical categories highlight the relation of a thing to its larger families and smaller subsets. Horizontal categories highlight different aspects of one thing. For example, a man can be vertically categorized as a human subset of animals and horizontally categorized by size, color, place, and talents. Vertical classification explores shared qualities of humans. Horizontal classification explores differences. These two categorization strategies became the foundation of modern observational disciplines such as botany, zoology, and psychology.

But vertical and horizontal categorization did not work well with ethics, poetry, and drama. When studying those fields, Aristotle experimented with different strategies, especially a combination of personal introspection and assessing common experiences. He analyzed his feelings as they were changed by literature or the theater, compared his own experience with others, and proposed ways of understanding these pursuits. When studying ethics and politics, he used a similar strategy of analyzing what constitutes happiness. Introspection and comparison with common experience were powerful tools of inquiry that are still at the foundation of some modern academic disciplines.

Aristotle thought about doing history in a manner that is of crucial importance to Christians. In a courtroom, the criminal case answers a historical problem: what happened? The evidence comes from eyewitnesses, chains of hearsay witnesses, documents, and, for Aristotle, even the testimony of people under torture. Aristotle recognized that the evidence comes from other people and that judgment is a social art. Personal observation, introspection, comparison with common experience, creating categories, and even syllogistic logic can't get you very far in either an ancient Greek court or a modern one. They can help, but what the court needs most is testimony: outside information brought into the jurisprudential process by witnesses. The academic discipline of history in Aristotelian tradition is a sort of collapsed courtroom. The historian acts as the judge (setting rules or evidence and procedure), prosecutor, and defender. The reader or listener is the jury. And, most importantly, the testimony is the basic information introduced. The historian and the listener/reader do not, and cannot, create the basic information. This information comes from an outside source. There is always one first question to ask before answering "Who stole the car?" "What happened between Julius Caesar and Cleopatra?" and "Did Jesus rise from the dead?" The first question is: "What information do we have from testifiers?"

Handling information from witnesses is a tool in Aristotle's pocketknife. For Aristotle, jurisprudence and history were awkward disciplines that depended on listening to and reading outside sources. History did not become a separate and independent discipline in universities until the nineteenth century, but the genre of writing history and the use of history in universities was long understood as a distinct practice of inquiry and judgment, different in method from biology or psychology and with different standards for "beyond reasonable doubt" and plausibility.

Aristotle's work as a historian is most evident in *Politics*. In the book, Aristotle is a voracious information gatherer. He studied histories of Greek cities and requested students and friends to supply him with information about the constitutions of other cities. Having no consistent information, he had to rely on anecdotes and examples to infer conclusions. The book ends in a weak and unfinished manner, concluding that there is no one system that fits all situations.

In his *Politics*, Aristotle is seen at his best. He really did try to figure something out, using all the tools available. In the end, the simple answer was not there. All he could offer were tentative conclusions and cobbled suggestion. Socrates or Plato could have never written a book like *Politics*. They would not have wanted to. They were true believers in forced simplification and grand pronouncement. Compare Aristotle's *Politics* and Plato's *Republic*. Aristotle had plenty of wacky thoughts while writing *Politics*, but it is a classic mishmash of a wise man doing the best he can to figure things out. In Aristotle is the intellectual vitality that drives universities.

Plato wrote literature that was saved and enjoyably read. Plato's stories of Socrates bantering with students have always been inspiring literature. On the other hand, nobody reads Aristotle for fun. Aristotle left behind books, lecture notes, and half-developed ideas that were buried after his death—purportedly to protect them. The Romans found the buried jumble not far from where Paul would be born. Roman educators became especially intrigued with Aristotle's most comprehensive intellectual strategy: *Topics*. This tool in the Aristotelian pocketknife is crucial for Christianity's place in modern universities and was the part of Aristotelian thinking most used by New Testament authors—especially Luke and Paul. *Topics* is a comprehensive schematic intellectual strategy that became the foundation for what came to be called "dialectic." Educated Romans like Luke and Paul were trained in dialectic as the structure of public reasonableness.

The most important first step in the schematic structure was to distinguish what was known by one's senses and by one's mind from what was learned from other people such as eyewitnesses and from hearsay reports both oral and written. Aristotle labels the former *technical* knowledge and the latter *non-technical* language. In Aristotelian thought over the next couple thousand years, it was always important to distinguish natural history as *technical* knowledge using *technical* methods and ancient human history as using *non-technical* methods. This distinction was crucial because, for example, the standards of evidence and who gets the benefit of the doubt are different in jurisprudence and human history than the standards of evidence in observational sciences such as biology.[6]

The New Testament authors, when making historical claims to Greek and Roman readers, relied on Aristotelian *Topics* and other Greek historical traditions. Cicero, Plutarch, and Quintilian, along with Christian intellectuals in the Roman Empire such as Luke, Clement, Eusebius, and Augustine, relied heavily on the system as the criterion of authoritative credibility. Aristotelian methods of thinking about history turned out to be of great use to Christianity because Christians needed a method to persuasively tell the history of Jesus, especially the multiple-eyewitnesses foundation to the resurrection.[7]

When Jesus humbled himself to become human, the act included humbling himself to have his resurrection seen by enough people for the event to attain not only local credibility but Greek-intellectual credibility. The sketch-lives of Jesus we call the gospels were not written to confirm to locals what they themselves had heard from Jesus in the Aramaic language. The gospels were written as missionary documents to be persuasive

---

6. This tradition of *Topics* is the subject of the book I was writing at the time of this trip, now published as *A History of Reasonableness: Testimony and Authority in the Art of Thinking*. See also Marincola, *Authority and Tradition*, 128–74.

7. Bauckham, *Jesus and the Eyewitnesses*.

among Greek-speaking, Greek-thinking people sprinkled from Britain to India, Africa, and Central Asia. Jesus, obligingly before his ascension, made sure there was a strong foundation of credible human testimony sufficient for the purposes of Greek-style history.

There are many Greek-academic tools of reasoning. Aristotle was not like Moses, giving law to Greek rationalism. He was a pocketknife kind of guy who tinkered with reasoning tools and strategies. He was amazingly broad-minded, the founding father to modern academic disciplines ranging from zoology to psychology to logic to politics to history. Christianity's best anchorages in universities are Aristotelian.

Having an anchorage, however, does not mean all anchorages are equal. Aristotle was a keen thinker about levels of certainty and differences in kinds of knowledge.

Not far southeast of us, at Bishop Pass, is Mount Agassiz, about fifty feet taller than Mount Darwin. Louis Agassiz was a professor at Harvard and probably the most famous natural historian in the world when Darwin's theory began to take hold in the 1860s. He was famous as an observer, categorizer, and fact-gatherer, compiling diverse information about glaciers and fish. It was Agassiz who gave us the term "Ice Age." Early on, Darwin looked up to Agassiz, and the two shared a desire to create grand theories about natural history. Eventually, though, the differences between the two became famous. Agassiz was unconvinced by Darwin's book. They wrote polite letters to each other, but each seems to have confused the other. Darwin thought Agassiz was stuck in the mud, and Agassiz thought Darwin a little over the top.

From 1871 to 1872, the aging Agassiz took an opportunity to go see the Galapagos Islands for himself. The U.S. Coast Survey needed to deliver a new scientifically-outfitted steamship to the West Coast, so they offered Agassiz and his wife to the opportunity to lead a group of "scientifics" on a study trip around Cape Horn. Agassiz decided he would reread Darwin's book and go see what Darwin saw. While in the Galapagos, Agassiz tried to have an open mind but ultimately remained unconvinced. The observable facts didn't fit together easily. He saw the diversity of finches; however, geologically, the islands were too young for the time required by Darwin's scenario of evolution to work. He died unconvinced, and his mountain does not overlook Evolution Valley.

Jesus, History, and Mount Darwin

To the north of us, overlooking Tioga Pass, is Mount Dana. James Dwight Dana was a natural historian at Yale slow to get on board with Darwin's theory. Like Wallace, Dana thought that evolution could not explain the complexities of the human mind. Eventually, Dana decided to provisionally accept Darwin's theory even though he remained a believer in divine revelation in the Bible. For Dana, random variation with natural selection wasn't a fully satisfying explanation for everything, but it served well as a best explanation for a lot of things.

The four of us, sweating through switchbacks, decided to take a rest. On a big rock, I laid out the map, compass, and altimeter/barometer and pointed to Mount Darwin in the distance. Dave looked at the map and compass and corrected me.

"No. That rise in the ridge next to it is Darwin."

Dave, Matt, and Steve

I, being his former professor, corrected his error. I checked the orientation of the map to magnetic north. Showed him, based on our elevation, where we were. If we were there on the map, then the real Darwin was at this angle from us.

Dave, a veteran of the first Gulf War whose Navy job was in the high-tech bowels of the aircraft carrier *Constellation*, was not impressed. "No. That one is Darwin."

"No," I replied. "Look at the way that rock points up. That is the pinnacle of Darwin."

"No. A little to the left is Darwin. What you are looking at is not the right pinnacle."

He wouldn't back down. This was mountain orienteering. I think I should have some authority here. As for Dave, yes, he had lots of training and experience with maps and instruments; however, it was *my* compass! We agreed to disagree. I gathered the tools of my leadership, and humped my pack onto my back.

Academic disciplines are not equal. At the great banquet table of the modern university, one of the hierarchical criteria assumed by many faculty members is that toward the head of the table are those disciplines that offer the strongest conclusions about the broadest and most important matters. Such disciplines have extraordinary confidence and freely engage in predicting the future, describing the past, and telling us what is going on at places no one has ever been. Physical sciences have this confidence when mathematically describing the formula for gravity or offering a model for how DNA works. The experiments, at best, are carefully constructed controlled experiences, the strongest of which produce the same results when repeated. After successfully predicting the outcome of an experiment, the scientist is justified to extrapolate his or her findings into the past and forward into the future. Repeatable events that can be precisely predicted are assumed to have always worked the same everywhere and will always work the same everywhere. A consistent train of experiments yields very high certainty when extrapolated out to universal applications. The strategy of contriving and extrapolating from multiple experiments was not invented by Aristotle but has become the most useful tool in the pocketknife-like collection of tools in the modern university. The strongest and most important theories of the physical sciences reach the status of "laws of nature."

In general, the physicists, chemists, molecular biologists, and other physical scientists of their type reign at the head of the great banquet table of academics. Other types of scientists, lesser sorts who can't control their experiments as well, range down the sides of the banquet table. Historians, philosophers, and literature professors usually find seats below the social sciences at the foot of the table.

Controlled experimentation and quantification are powerful tools that Aristotle never explored. In modern universities, academic disciplines that can use experiments and quantification are respected and given higher seats at the university banquet.

Aristotle knew math but did not conceive the range of usefulness that mathematics would develop. Disciplines that can quantify, measure, and rise from individual instance to formulaic models fill the middle ranks of the university banquet. Social sciences have grown up out of what were formerly weak fields to become capable of predicting, with high probability, future events. Even the discipline of history has sought quantification when it can. Anything quantifiable becomes available for modeling. Data on the quantifiable aspects of marriage and family life, if a historian can find enough of it, produce patterns that help us make strong inferences about seemingly unrelated matters.

John Henry Newman, one of the most thoughtful churchmen in English history, proclaimed in his *Idea of the University* (1852) that theologians should be sitting at the head of the table, guiding the university disciplines so as to teach *universal* knowledge. "Is not the being of a God reported to us by testimony, handed down by history, inferred by an inductive process, brought home to us by metaphysical necessity, urged on us by the suggestions of our conscience?"[8] These three sitting together—to the right the book of testimony, to the left the book of nature, in the middle Queen Theology—would host the university banquet. "University Teaching without Theology is simply unphilosophical."[9]

In Newman's university one discipline would coordinate and rule over all the others. Theology would make sense of biology. Essentially, Newman was a *Totalizer* like the modern biologists who say Darwinism

---

8. Newman, *Idea of the University*, 25.
9. Ibid., 42.

should rule over theology. In actual practice, no discipline rules and coordinates all the others. There is a hierarchical university banquet, but the head of the table does not rule over the foot. The head of the table goes to disciplines with the highest claims to important certainties and the ability to produce more certainties. At the foot of the table are historians who can offer, at best, plausible and persuasive information and assessments about non-repeatable events. But we at the foot of the table have our rightful place.

I don't use quantification or statistics for the kind of history I do, but I am amazed by their powers and uses. Huge matters often hang from mere statistical probabilities. When the boys each needed their baby shots, a nurse handed me a clipboard with a waiver for me to sign informing me of the chance that my child would die from the shot. The mathematics of chance is about groups more than individuals, but here my child became an individual toss of the coin. Public policy required the shot, an informed parent, and the legal release of responsibility. Two numbers in the ratio could be my boy's future—one number being the more likely. Each time I went to the county clinic for the shots, I would sign the waiver, hold my son on my lap, cringe while the nurse shot him in the thigh, and hope I was not helping my son's executioner.

My dad was a weatherman in the Navy in the era before satellites and super computers. Meteorologists are a combination of mathematician, historian, and fortune-teller. Society wants them to be wizard-like advisors, but they do best to stay humble with their conclusions. Their data only goes a limited distance into the past, and they can predict the future only so far out. The contingencies of weather can change at any minute. Meteorology is the most humble of quantifiable earth sciences. But when it is working within its limits, it is very powerful.

In the late 1950s my dad was stationed on the aircraft carrier *Princeton* in the western Pacific as part of a fleet led by the *Lexington*. Dad, doing his job, predicted that a typhoon was headed toward the fleet. The *Lexington's* weathermen, however, were not predicting the typhoon. Dad reported his weather predictions to his superiors on the *Princeton*, warning them of the coming storm. The admiral on the *Princeton* then radioed to the fleet admiral. Dad was just a twenty-something lieutenant doing math-modeling, but soon an entire fleet of United States warships turned westward steaming at full speed for the Bashi Channel of the Philippines to get leeward of Luzon. The typhoon came, and the kid-officer with a slide-rule was the hero.

Of course, not all his predictions came true. A good weatherman can't get cocky. When I was growing up, our family sometimes wanted him to use his expertise and give us a weather forecast. He never would with any confidence. He would beg ignorance. There were too many variables, and he did not have enough information.

Geologist and evolutionary biologists are not as humble as meteorologists. They tend to put more confidence in their models. Darwin's study of evolutionary biology was deeply influenced by a new model of geology that de-emphasized random, individual catastrophes and, instead, emphasized long, general, stable changes traceable in the earth's past and predictive into the future. At the time, this type of geology was called *uniformitarianism*. Darwin's friend and mentor, Charles Lyell, was the most famous proponent of *uniformitarianism*. Lots of scientists loved Lyell and the surveyors of the Sierra Nevada sprinkled his name prominently. If you walk east out of the Yosemite and Tuolumne Valleys on the John Muir Trail, you come to the Lyell Fork of the Tuolumne River. Walking south from this confluence, you follow the Lyell Fork through Lyell Canyon headed toward Mount Lyell (13,114′). Eventually the trail takes you into Evolution Valley.

Charles Lyell (1797–1875) was one of the pleasant gentlemen of wealth and leisure who helped create modern science. Charles Darwin excitedly received the second volume of Lyell's *Principles of Geology* (vol. 1: 1830, vol. 2: 1832) while on board the *Beagle*. Lyell, as a young man, enjoyed botany and entomology, but while at Oxford in 1817 he attended lectures on mineralogy and geology that encouraged him to a lifelong devotion to earth science. Lyell was not so leisured that he did not want a career, but he was rich enough not to have to live off his income as a lawyer. Mostly, he and his wife enjoyed traveling and geologizing. He also gained some fame as a proponent of curriculum reform advocating more science education.

Lyell's grand theory of *uniformitarianism* was the belief that the answers to geological questions about the deep past could be found in observation of the present. The earth's conditions were stable through time, so the changes evident in the earth's surface were the result of the long, slow, and incremental work of geological forces. Catastrophes and other one-time actions—especially any individual actions by divine intervention—were discounted as unimportant in the long run. When Lyell emphasized the steadiness of nature over vast amounts of time, analogy became the most important historical tool: the distant past is analogous to the local present.

Many successes in the field of geology are rooted in Lyell's method of analogy. In 1834, Lyell went to Sweden to study whether the land there was actually rising. He found evidence that it was and, by making an analogy, he assumed that such rising and sinking of land was a slow process happening all around the globe. Lyell inspired young Darwin. When in South America in 1836, Darwin discovered evidence that South America was experiencing elevation changes and wrote a paper supporting Lyell's speculations. Lyell's textbook taught students such as Darwin not to ask questions about the mysteries of God's past interaction with the world, but instead look for slow physical laws at work.

The trouble with *uniformitarianism* is not that it is wrong, but that it is not always right. Emphasis on the steady has proven to be tremendously useful in natural history. However, it is not always helpful. The realities of nature for which we have direct recent evidence can be puzzlingly unpredictable.

Stopping for another rest along the trail, I pulled out my topographical map, compass, and altimeter/barometer. Matthew and Steven studiously avoided showing any interest. They have suffered through too many sermons about how bad maps give too little information, better maps give lots of information, and the best maps show how unstable the information is. University classrooms are like maps. The best classes on anything should inspire a student with the instability of knowledge.

"Nature is messy," a geologist at University of California, Davis tells writer John McPhee. "Don't expect it to be uniform or consistent."[10] McPhee's books on geology tend to emphasize the humbling effect of the real earth on the over-intellectual geologists who want to over-simplify it. In *Rising from the Plains* (1986), McPhee rambles through Wyoming with an aging U.S. Geological Survey geologist who heaps disdain on

---

10. McPhee, *Assembling California*, 24.

"Megathinkers" who don't get dirty working in the field. Field geologists have to be more humble and face everyday the quirky and irregular aspects of places like Wyoming. The government, however, is downsizing the regional offices. "The name of the game now is 'modelling,' on office computers at the national office." He describes modelers as working in a "black box" where the earth becomes an abstraction and the awkward individual facts evident in the field get smoothed over.[11]

Maps are abstractions. Maps are intellectual models. We all learn in school that maps are necessarily inaccurate. We learn that it is geometrically impossible to take a three-dimensional sphere and put it on a two-dimensional surface. Not even globes are accurate because the earth isn't a sphere. Every map or globe has to make trade-offs with reality. Even with all our high-tech satellites and computer graphics, we can't overcome the problems of first-year geometry. But as with most things in our middling existence between knowledge and mystery, we are practical people. If it works, then we focus on what we can do, not what we can't. In history classes about early America, it is common to smile at the Northwest Ordinance that cut up the lands above the Ohio River with a flat grid pattern. With no concern for the actual topography of the land or the curvature of the earth, our government established two-dimensional order on a three-dimensional complexity. Any kid with a sphere can tell you that north-south lines converge. No government can decree that the land can be distributed with grid-like equality of squares. I used to live in Indiana. The grids, after fiddling by surveyors, loosely work. They function well enough, so we move on.

Global positioning system (GPS) units are dangerous for how little information they give about their weaknesses. GPS units inspire people to raptures of amazement that the little screen shows their position exactly on the earth—give or take a few feet. However, a GPS unit calculates its position by triangulation with several satellites, and then correlates that position to a map in its memory—not to the actual earth. Good boating classes in coastal navigation remind students not to place too much trust in the GPS. Looking at the GPS screen is not the same as looking at reality.

To get really picky, the GPS unit does not work directly with the actual shape of the earth. The earth is slightly flattened. GPS uses an ideal

---

11. McPhee, *Rising from the Plains*, 148–49.

sphere as a model upon which it imposes circular latitude and longitude lines. When a handheld GPS calculates its position by latitude and longitude—which is its best work—it is not calculating its place actually on earth. It is calculating its place on a sphere that is a close representation of a non-spherical earth. This is one of the reasons a GPS will always be slightly imprecise. As with most things, the further we dig, the more squishy our knowledge.

There is also the problem that true north and magnetic north are not stable. *Longitude* (1995) tells the story of making clocks that would work at sea to help sailors calculate their position east and west. The book fits the standard model for histories of science: the triumph of knowledge over ignorance, human ingenuity causing progress, the scientist as hero. What few people seem to realize is that latitude is a harder problem than longitude. Calculating longitude was a human problem solved by doing what humans do best: inventing. A better clock was invented. Latitude, however, is an earth problem. Trouble is: the earth is messy and not cooperative.

The earth is elastic in erratic ways. Not only is the earth's shape and distribution of its mass not stable, the earth also wobbles, causing the north and south poles to wobble. The poles don't wander too far, but with poles whose positions aren't stable, we can't have precise latitude on maps, because latitude is an angle measured from the north or south pole. The problem affects astronomers and such things as the target systems inside intercontinental ballistic missiles. Today there is an International Terrestrial Reference Frame that uses computer models to quantitatively estimate polar motion and its effects. We still can only estimate the future latitude of a point on earth and any map is accurate only within a range of unknowing.[12]

---

12. See Carter and Carter, *Latitude: How American Astronomers Solved the Mystery of Variation*. Note that the mystery solved in the subtitle is the mystery of what was happening, not the mystery that it happens.

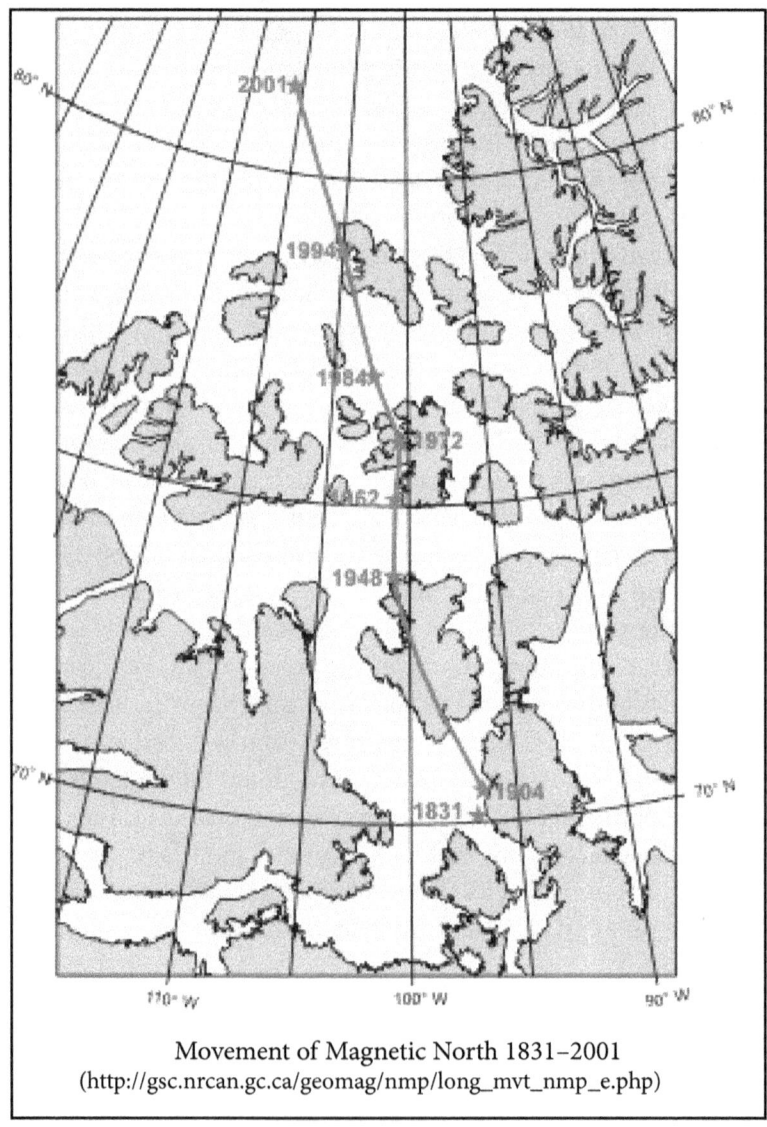

Movement of Magnetic North 1831–2001
(http://gsc.nrcan.gc.ca/geomag/nmp/long_mvt_nmp_e.php)

Magnetic north is also problematic. The first thing to do with a map is to use a compass and information on the map to orient magnetic north to true north. Good maps tell you the average magnetic variation for a general region for the publication year of that map. Extremely good maps such as nautical charts from the National Oceanographic and Atmospheric Administration (NOAA) tell you the yearly rate of variation change and have lots of information about areas of magnetic disturbance where your compass will not work. All these maps go bad after a few years. There is a short window of accuracy to the maps and their magnetic predictions. Magnetic north wanders erratically. Every day it wanders over a region of about 85 km. Year to year, it heads in a generally northwest direction. Also, the intensity of its force is diminishing. There is a possibility that it might flip-flop soon, as it has done erratically in the past, thus causing all compass needles to go through a period of pointing nowhere and eventually pointing south instead of north.

Most GPS units confidently tell you the latitude and ask you, with no qualms, whether you want magnetic or true north. To be precise: this is smoke and mirrors. The true north it gives you is one that correlates to a spherical abstraction in the unit, not to the real north that is wobbling. The magnetic north it offers is just a rough calculation based on an average variation for some usually unstated date. The GPS does not take into account that magnetic north is unpredictably wandering; therefore, the further from the date of the map calculation—which is usually much older than the date of purchasing the GPS—the more your GPS is just guessing.

Your GPS is not dangerous to use. It is only dangerous to be overconfident about what it tells you. For Dave and me, with our maps and compass laid out on a rock, the weaknesses of our information are not a problem. Navigating in the High Sierra is pretty simple. The deep assumptions and problems submerged in my map won't affect us. On the other hand, knowledge of its deep assumptions and instabilities can encourage a little humility and care along the way.

Much that goes on in universities is like what goes on inside a GPS unit. We find it useful to create models, and then study the models as reality. However, all members of universities should strive to be wise about keeping "useful" separate from "true." At universities, we are supposed to try and hold to them both. We get into trouble when we assume that they are identical or only care about one or the other.

At noon we reached Blue Lake at 10,400 feet. We were through the worst of the switchbacks and were seeing an increasing amount of snow and ice. I kept an eye on the barometer, looking for trends that would show a change in the weather. We had a high-pressure air mass over us the whole weekend, keeping bad weather away and blue skies above, but I watched barometric pressure anyway as we were going up. We were climbing late in the season, and big mountains can create their own weather. If the barometric pressure started dropping faster than it should with the higher altitude, we would be looking at rain or snow. Though Blue Lake was pleasantly surrounded by trees, we were headed up above tree-line where we could see only chunks of rock.

Up close, the High Sierra ridges are not pretty. The High Sierra is being violently pushed up as California, geologically, keeps jamming itself into Nevada. These mountains are young and not smoothed by old age. To the west, the Sierra foothills crumple as California crushes into Nevada. The eastern face is pushed more forcefully up, creating a wall of peaks over 14,000 feet high. Mount Lassen and Mount Shasta in northern California are volcanoes sitting grandly isolated. Approaching from the west, it is easier to see that Mount Darwin and Mount Mendel are really just two high spots on a long high ridge. Maybe this is appropriate because Mendel, the person, doesn't stand alone in history. His importance, unbeknownst to him, is as an independent researcher who hit upon something needed desperately by Darwin.

Approaching from the east, we won't see Mount Mendel (13,710′) until we are on the ridge leading to Darwin's summit. Theodore Solomons, when naming the Evolution Group in 1895, did not name Mount Mendel. At that time, Gregor Mendel (1822–1884) was unknown to all but a tiny few scientists. He is considered the father of genetics, the field that, more than any other, has partnered up with Darwinism in mutual confirmation and explanation. The peak's name was proposed by the Sierra Club in 1942. The peak had not been named earlier because many thought the peak was already named after Alfred Russell Wallace. But Wallace had another peak. Even the 1912 and 1918 USGS maps misnamed the peak. So when the confusion was worked out, there was an unnamed summit next to Mount Darwin. With genetics growing and elementary textbooks praising Mendel as a model scientist performing a model experiment, his was the perfect name for the mountain.

Mendel died two years after Darwin. At his death he was abbot of an Augustinian monastery in Brno, north of Vienna, in what is today the Czech Republic. It was not until 1900 that Mendel's scientific work was discovered by men in search of an experimental way to see Darwin's mechanism of selection at work. Darwin had merely speculated that there must be some physical point in reproduction where traits are passed to the next generation with a possibility of random variation. Darwin never saw a gene or knew about the replicating structure of DNA's double helix; the field of genetics did not develop until the 1950s. Between the publication of Darwin's book in 1859 and the publication of James Watson and Francis Crick's description of DNA in 1953, the best support of Darwin's theory was Mendel's experiment with peas in his monastery garden.

The discovery of Mendel's work was a boon to those who wanted to promote Darwinian speculations in the down-to-earth mechanical manner of experimental science. Robin Marantz Henig opens her biography, *The Monk in the Garden: The Lost and Found Genius of Gregor Mendel the Father of Genetics* (2000), with an account of the excitement of Cambridge zoologist William Bateson in 1900 upon realizing that Mendel had a *controlled, experimental* method to get at what Darwin only observed in the wild. Mendel found a multi-generational, mathematically understandable pattern in peas that enhanced the conviction that there was a physical mechanism in living things acting as a shuffler of traits. Mendel's experiments did not prove *randomness*, but they did show that a variation and selection process was happening with mathematical consistency.

Of course, Mendel was a Christian, an Augustinian monk. Mendel wrote nothing about the religious implications he drew from his experiments; however, we can suppose that he handled it in the typical manner of folks who follow St. Augustine: God is the creator, sovereign, and purpose-giver to all creation. God likes humans to be creative, inquisitive, and rational.

While it is doubtful Mendel would have been interested in Darwin's negative theology, Mendel's work came to be the scientific bridge from Darwinian speculations to laboratory genetics. Darwin speculated, Mendel saw more, and genetics found the physical mechanism necessary for variation and sexual selection. Nobody proved or disproved anything about God or randomness.

The story of Mendel is also an inspiring picture of the scientist as monk—devoted, diligent, disciplined, and patient. Mendel and Darwin could be partnered up in textbooks as model scientists, one in a monastery garden, and the other on the Galapagos Islands, both seeking neither fame nor power nor grants nor even university advancement; instead, they sought with simplicity the truths of nature.

Gregor Mendel, a farmer's son who had done acceptable work in school, entered the Augustinian order, a monastic tradition known for its scholarly mission and excellence, at the age of twenty-one. Mendel had scholarly aspirations but earned weak test scores and often suffered debilitating depression. He was long denied entrance to the university in Vienna. However in 1850, at the extreme age of twenty-eight, he gained the sympathy of university examiners and his abbot, who thought it good to give him a chance to further his education. Mendel showed no brilliance at the university, but did enjoy science, counting things, and keeping track of measurements.

After returning to the monastery from the university in 1853, Mendel's abbot assigned him to teach science at a public school. Mendel apparently enjoyed the work as a teacher and further appointed himself town weatherman. He loved the daily collection of weather data and eventually published an article on the subject. His only other publication was a paper he read to the town's science club on the generational patterns of hybrid peas. His life of science was cut short by becoming an administrator. In 1868, he was elected abbot of his monastery.

Mendel was not all that smart, but he had characteristics better than smart: he was diligent, patient, and skillful. He was also lucky. The peas he chose to study were perfectly suited to giving the outcome he got. One of the few naturalists who would design to correspond with Mendel was a professor named Nägeli who also worked with hybridization. (Darwin had written a chapter on hybridization in *Origin of Species,* and Mendel sent him a copy of his published paper; however, Darwin never took the time even to glance at Mendel's work. The article remained in Darwin's papers with uncut pages.) Nägeli responded to Mendel's desire to correspond with authoritative naturalists, but Nägeli primarily studied hawkweed, a plant that was more complex than peas. Nägeli's work had long been frustrated by the plant on which he worked. Mendel's plant made seeing the patterns easier.

Dave and I wanted to get over to the top of Mount Mendel, but it seemed unlikely that we would have time on this trip. Standing on the summit of Mount Darwin *and* Mount Mendel would be a thrill. The two together are more meaningful than either separate.

Base Camp

At Blue Lake we had lunch and rested. The boys were happy. Dave and I chatted. Eventually we gathered our gear and started walking, Matt up ahead with Steve and me in back. The trail was now less steep.

Richard Dawkins, in *Climbing Mount Improbable*, creates a parable of a mountain climb to answer the mathematical problem with Darwinian natural history. The mathematical problem of Darwinian natural history is portrayed in Dawkins' book as a steep cliff that blocks climbers from getting to the top. Dawkins recognizes that genetics may have found DNA and people can watch in laboratories the process of variation and sexual selection, but also acknowledges a problem with the mathematics. There does not seem to be enough time in earth's history to allow enough random variation through sexual selection to create complicated things like the human brain. The math in natural history is a daunting problem that he depicts as a steep cliff.

There are various ways to handle this mathematical problem. "Chaos theory" posits the possibility of fast spurts of variation and selection. Theories of multiple universes allow us to spread the mathematics broader so that the calculations of random variation work. The idea that Dawkins likes best emphasizes algorithms. In Dawkins's parable, an easy trail, the algorithm, winds up the back of the mountain, avoiding the mathematical cliff. The randomness in random variation is not really random, because variation is affected by algorithmic "pressure."

Daniel Dennett, in *Darwin's Dangerous Idea* (1995), describes Darwinian evolution as "algorithmic sorting processes, which take the probabilities or biases that are due to fundamental laws of physics and produce structures that would otherwise be wildly improbable."[13] An algorithm is a closed information system in which infinite possibilities are honed into a finite form by the action of a recurring set of rules. Algorithms domesticate wildness. Modern computers, the World Wide Web, and hopes for continuing development of artificial intelligence are rooted in the wonders of algorithms. Probably nothing in mathematics is so inspirational to futurists as the idea that algorithms seem to make simple the complex. David Berlinski, in his breathless *The Advent of the Algorithm: The Idea that Rules the World* (2000), writes that after Newton's

---

13. Dennett, *Darwin's Dangerous Idea*, 162.

calculus, the algorithm "is the second great scientific idea of the West. There is no third."[14]

Limited time is a problem for natural history. Louis Agassiz could not accept Darwinian evolution because he thought the islands of the Galapagos were geologically too young for the mathematics of chance variations being sexually selected. Dawkins points out that "if Darwinism were really a theory of chance, it couldn't work."[15] Dawkins believes "Darwinism is *not* a theory of random chance. It is a theory of random mutation plus *non-random* cumulative natural selection."[16]

The possibility that algorithmic pressures affect natural history solves some problems but raises others. Not the least of these problems is: how does the algorithm get started? If algorithms work from rules, where do the rules come from?

Huffing my way to Mount Darwin, I was dealing with the real earth and a real mountain. I found little joy in thinking about stories of an easy trail round back dependent on algorithms. But hey, I am the guy who thinks nature is wild and that God created time in convoluted ways. Who knows the fullness of creation? God may have created an algorithm to help variation and selection. As an academic historian, I take heart in Dawkins' stretch to algorithms. It shows a major problem in natural history that can't be answered easily.

Out there on the trail up to a real Mount Darwin, I was free to let my mind wander. Time is a wonder. Math is a wonder. On the other hand, Steven was having a tougher time getting up the mountain than I had expected. He wasn't up front as he normally was on hikes. He was holding us back. I began to doubt whether we would be able to make it to the top of the mountain. It was cold. The air was getting thinner. We were moving slowly. Time was not on our side.

We arrived at Midnight Lake at 3 PM and found a site for base camp on a rise at the northeast end about twenty five yards from shore. We were alone above tree-line with steep granite all around us except for the canyon through which we had just hiked. We slumped our packs against a rock and surveyed the lake in its rocky basin. Steve hit me with a snowball. I

---

14. Berlinski, *Advent of the Algorithm*, xvi.
15. Dawkins, *Climbing Mount Improbable*, 77.
16. Ibid., 75.

told him he would sleep in fear. The sun would soon be falling behind the high western ridge, so by 3:30 PM I started boiling water while Dave and the kids set up the two tents. After organizing his gear, Dave took over the cooking duties.

With the four of us huddled next to a rock, we discussed the decisions to be made for the next day. We needed to be back to the car before dark because we were not sure it would actually run, given the fact that it wasn't getting out of first gear when we parked it. Tomorrow, if we were up and hiking by dawn, we would have four or so hours to climb a little less than three thousand feet. It would be doable if the kids caught the spirit in the morning. We would leave most of our gear here, and the kids would carry nothing. While Dave continued to cook, Matt got the radio out of my pack. We had no idea whether the radio would work in such canyons, but the pre-game chatter should have started. I fiddled with the knobs and could not pick up a sports station. Dave, in U.S. Navy mode, taught Matt to say in such a situation, "No joy on the comms!"

After dinner the temperature dropped fast. The shadow of the western ridge climbed the wall behind us as we looked over the lake toward the steep canyon that led up to Blue Heaven Lake, at the base of Mount Darwin. I was anxious to get to the top. I wanted to stand on the summit of Darwin and look over at Mendel and the other peaks, especially Fiske, one of the few mountains named after an American historian.

Dave, who is the best of hiking buddies, full of wit and energy, wrote in my pocket notebook:

> 17:02 hrs
> NOTE: Previous attempt at comms resulting in no joy was due to operator error. A formal investigation will be conducted at a later time, along with remedial training and disciplinary action.

Matt had found the World Series on the radio. It was now so cold we all decided to huddle into my two-person tent to play cards and listen to the game. My two sons and a good friend and I were deep in sleeping bags playing cards in a tiny tent while listening to the Giants win a well-played game. Cards and baseball are the fun of mathematics combined with the wildness of being human. We laughed and yelled. We shivered. It was great.

4

Mount Darwin

There are actually two Mount Darwins. We woke up to climb the second one. The first Mount Darwin was named in honor of the budding scientist's twenty-fifth birthday. He wasn't even *the* Charles Darwin yet when he got his first mountain. Captain FitzRoy of the *HMS Beagle*, when surveying Tierra del Fuego and anchored in Ponsonby Sound, looked out on some sharp peaks in the distance and named the tallest one for his sailing companion as a birthday present. I suppose you have to be a British naval officer at the height of the empire to be that presumptuous. Theodore Solomons was less cavalier when naming mountains. But naming mountains still seems a bit presumptuous. This morning we were at the base of Solomons' Mount Darwin—the tallest peak in the Evolution Range.

In deep Sierra canyons, the sun does not warm things up till late. Dawn is just the brightening of the sky. It was 28°F outside the tents when I got water boiling. We stood around the stove eating oatmeal as I read our Sunday morning lesson from Colossians 1:15–17:

> Christ is the image of the invisible God, the firstborn over all creation. For by him all things were created: things in heaven and on earth, visible and invisible, whether thrones or powers or rulers or authorities; all things were created by him and for him. He is before all things, and in him all things hold together.

After prayer we began to pick our way up and over to the shoulder of a ridge where, at about 11,400 feet, where we would be able to see Mount Darwin. Dave and I carried daypacks and the kids were just in their sweatshirts. No one else was around. It looked like we would be alone going up the mountain.

Mount Darwin

✣ ✣ ✣

The first known ascent of Mount Darwin was in 1908, by three geologists studying ice action: Grove Karl Gilbert, Willard D. Johnson, and E. C. Andrews. Leaving the University of California, Berkeley on July 31, they approached the Evolution Group from the west. Andrews wrote an account of their trip for the *Sierra Club Bulletin:*

> As we approached the district, we noted, far away on the horizon, perhaps as much as sixty miles distant in front of us, an immense mass, presenting a wonderful aréte along the skyline. Johnson, who knew I was anxious to climb a high mountain, thereupon drew my attention to this formidable pile, and suggested that its ascent would furnish a good alpine scramble. I replied, "It is the roughest mountain in the whole landscape," to which he replied in turn, "That is the very reason why I would suggest its ascent. It is Mount Darwin ... and not yet ascended."[1]

The Pinnacle of Mt. Darwin, photographed by Richard M. Leonard. Thanks to the Colby Memorial Library, Sierra Club for the use of its historial archives.

1. Andrews, "First Ascent of Mount Darwin—1908."

Setting up a base camp at Evolution Lake, they scrambled up the western face to the chimney on the ridge that we were headed toward from the east. They did not carry ropes and the chimney was slippery from ice. "The frost," Andrews wrote, "was almost our undoing from the start." But soon they reached "a very small area which constituted the main summit." Gilbert and Johnson were happy to get to where they were, but Andrews wanted to climb the nearby pinnacle that was obviously the real summit, a few feet higher than the summit plateau. Andrews made his way down another chimney and over to where he "then made use of a monstrous icicle one foot in diameter to assist me in climbing the broken masonry of the outstanding peak." Sitting on the summit, he realized that "the descent was more perilous than the ascent, especially as I had the terrible abyss below in full view the whole time that I was rounding the crag." With the thought of falling a couple of thousand feet, Andrews dropped down to the narrow ledge six or seven feet below and climbed back over to where his two companions were watching.

This was why I was carrying climbing equipment. To get my kids up through the chimney, especially if there was any ice, and then to the top of the pinnacle, I wanted the security of good rope and good knots. On the other hand, I would not be surprised to find the climb easier than they described. Climbers tend to over-write their accomplishments. Darwin is not the Matterhorn or the Eiger. The *Sierra Club Bulletin* published a picture in 1934 of the pinnacle showing that it was formidable, but accompanying the picture were the mountaineering notes of a club outing in 1933 base-camped at Evolution Lake. Twenty men and nine women summited Darwin that year.[2]

Summiting is, to use the cliché, a mountain-top experience. Darwin assumed that "everyone must know the feeling of triumph and pride which a grand view from a height communicates to the mind."[3] Summits encourage mountaineers to wax metaphysical. Henry Thoreau wrote about climbing Mount Katahdin in Maine:

> The tops of mountains are among the unfinished parts of the globe, whither it is a slight insult to the gods to climb and pry into their secrets, and try their effect on our humanity. Only daring and

2. Dawson, "Mountain-Climbing," 92–95.
3. Darwin, *Voyage of the Beagle*, 298.

insolent men, perchance, go there. Simple races, as savages, do not climb mountains,—their tops are sacred and mysterious tracts never visited by them. Pomola is always angry with those whom climb to the summit of Ktaadn.[4]

In 1921 Chester Rowell, a regent of the University of California and editor of the *San Francisco Chronicle,* declared in a speech to fellow members of the Sierra Club:

> A great peak is a frowning challenge, until we have scaled it; a strong and trusted friend thereafter. We can share the life of the mountain; we can search its history until we are as old in knowledge as it is in experience; we can stand on its summit and be lifted in spirit as if we had grown to its height and expanded in soul to the whole reach of a broadened horizon. The glaciers have carved a castle for us whose ceiling the sun emblazons with cubic miles of filmy gold; the winds fling banners from the bleak peaks; the winters of ages have piled out partitions; the summer of centuries have grown the pines for our bedposts, and God has scattered the firmament with stars, to give us courage by contemplating their infinity, to measure our pygmy finitude against the giant but also finite mountains. The torrents and the pines sing to us, the birds and busy squirrels speak to us, the rocks preach to us, and the mind is at stress with muscles as the soul breathes deep with the lungs. So the mountains enter into our lives as we enter into theirs. We are lifted up in the high places, not beyond ourselves, but to our best selves.[5]

Rowell carries the reader up to the summit with him. Summits are romantic. They make people feel good about God, themselves, and nature.

❖ ❖ ❖

Jesus was transfigured in glory on the summit of a mountain. Tradition puts him on the impressive little hill called Mount Tabor (1,843′); however, since the gospels call it a "high mountain," some people have preferred to think of Jesus being transfigured on Mount Hermon, the tallest mountain in Israel (9,230′). Whichever mountain it occurred upon, the event lacked romance. At the summit, Peter wants to turn the event into some sort of worship moment, but God is short and snippy. Out of a cloud

---

4. Thoreau, *Maine Woods,* 641.
5. Rowell, "Mountain and the Sea," 502.

God interrupts to give Peter, James, and John one short directive: "This is my Son, whom I love; listen to him."[6]

History is an academic discipline founded upon listening. More than any other intellectual strategy, history uses listening in order to get at the past—especially to get at the individuals who spoke and did specific things. Psychoanalysis uses listening too, but is especially oriented to hearing what is not being said. Many historians have sadly been taught to listen with a cynical ear. Certainly listening to hearsay reports is always tricky.

Thucydides reminds readers that the speeches in his book are actually short accounts of speeches.[7] We teachers have to remind students that ancient books did not use quotation marks. There is no account of an ancient speech, conversation, or advice that should be taken as the literal words spoken. The constraints of writing a book about long events usually make it practical for an author to not even try to give a whole or exact transcript of a speech. The Sermon on the Mount certainly lasted longer than the 10–15 minutes it takes to read out loud. And Jesus surely did not preach in Greek.

On the other hand, we historians who are not overly cynical still listen carefully for authentic ideas, words, commands, conversations, and even complex political or religious speeches that we believe are embedded in the hearsay of our authors, even our ancient authors. We can hear Pericles within Thucydides' account of Pericles' funeral oration in Athens. It fits with what we know about Pericles. Thucydides has earned our trust throughout the whole of his book. We understand that Thucydides has written a highly organized book; though it has a specific agenda, he is giving his readers true information. Pericles's oration artfully illuminates Athenian political ideals, imperial perspectives, and deep antagonism to Sparta. The authentic event bubbles up, allowing us today to listen to Pericles.

Ancient historians have to have ears to hear. Natural history, Darwin's kind of history, is mostly a discipline of observation and extrapolation by analogy from present observation to the deep past. Natural historians don't listen so much as look. The natural sciences have observational methods to get at the deep past. The discipline doesn't, as a rule, listen to ancient people reporting about the more ancient past. Darwin was a

---

6. Mark 9:7. Luke 9:35 and Matthew 17:5 have the same beginning and ending, but different middles.

7. Thucydides, *Peloponnesian War*, I.22.

great natural historian who did not practice human history. Christianity is about human history, the story of God's interactions with people of ancient West Asia. Darwin on the Galapagos observed nothing that necessarily affects what a historian hears about a man who claimed to be God in ancient Palestine. Natural history can observe gravity at work and appropriately assume that gravity worked two thousand years ago as it does today; however, to know that Jesus defied gravity and walked on water, one has to move from natural history to ancient history, from observation and extrapolation to listening and believing.

Jesus told his disciples to "consider carefully how you listen."[8] The "how" in that sentence is important. With what attitude do you listen? With how much openness do you listen? Do you listen with a cynical ear? How much are you willing to believe? Who gets the benefit of the doubt? Are you fundamentally optimistic or pessimistic about whether the truth is coming down to us through time in documents and by hearsay witnesses?

Aristotle is again my guide. Aristotle optimistically believed that truth is stronger than error. At the beginning of his *Art of Rhetoric*, Aristotle taught that truth, ultimately, is more persuasive than its opposite. "Truth is not beyond human nature," wrote Aristotle, "and men do, for the most part, achieve it."[9] Aristotelian optimism is a tradition in many university disciplines. University disciplines generally assume that they are on the right track and that, over the long run, knowledge and understanding are progressing. Lots of professors like to act cynical because they think this makes them seem wise, but most university professors are deeply optimistic.

The Aristotelian tradition values long periods of time and much social interaction because it asserts that truth is best discerned generally but not necessarily individually. If large numbers of reasonable people, especially those recognized for wisdom and discernment, agree over long periods of time on the authority of statements of wisdom and information, then there is a good chance truth is in the wisdom and information. Truth will out. Truth is stronger and more lasting than error.

Christians have long associated this with the work of the Holy Spirit. The Bible books were gathered together and core church doctrines

---

8. Luke 8:18.
9. Aristotle, *Art of Rhetoric*, 68–69, 1355a.

developed over several hundred years out of the interactions of diverse peoples, institutions, and cultures. Christians, many of whom appreciated Aristotle's teachings, have long gloried in the authority that comes from social consensus through time. This does not mean that errors do not proliferate in time, but it does mean that the benefit of the doubt should go to information being passed down through history that has the momentum of great consensus. Herodotus wrote of having an "obligation" to such information and Augustine wrote of "submission" to it.[10]

I have academic friends who are surprised that I actually believe Jesus said, in his own language, "consider carefully how you listen." They think it philosophically naïve, to say nothing of lacking proper critical understanding of the gospels. When I say that I believe Jesus actually walked on water and rose from the dead, these friends tell me that such statements are not statements of history; they are something else. I had a friend tell me that historical testimony about the resurrection is "a spectacle refracted through my present longings and interests," needing my mind to give it truth, offering me an opportunity to create a historical foundation for Christianity.

R.G. Collingwood, in *The Idea of History* (1946), is the most influential philosopher of history to insist that history is in the historian's mind. Collingwood attacked the notion that history is mostly about reasonable use of what Aristotelian tradition called "ready made" information—ready made because it comes *to* a historian already having form and shape. Collingwood attacked this tradition. He wanted historians to be lone wolf detectives, not members of a social studies discipline. Collingwood insisted that history was individual and mental rather than social and out-there.[11]

Here I stand with Darwin. The two of us are historians who believe that the history we study really is out there. True events in history are true, not because we, today, think them true, but because they happened. I want to reach the summit of Mount Darwin, not to throw Darwin off the mountain, but to stand next to him. We have different methods, but

---

10. For examples, see Herodotus, *Histories*, VII. 152. and Augustine, *On Christian Doctrine*, II.vii.10.

11. See the chapter on Collingwood in Coady's *Testimony*, and Kennedy's *History of Reasonableness*, 227–40.

both of us are keen to use what evidence is available to us in order to get at what actually happened. Neither of us wants to play mind games.

In the cold morning air with the sun not yet over the ridge, the place to begin is with miracles. If Christianity is false, vain, and a sham, if Jesus did not rise from the dead, then Christianity's viability in discussion at the great university banquet table hinges on the ability of historians to study miracles. But how should we as academic historians study miracles? The past and the present are awash in reports of seemingly incredible events.

Modern academic tradition tends to try and maintain order. For historians, this means refusing to listen to reports of what are generally called miracles. David Hume founded this modern avoidance method in *Of Miracles*, printed in *Enquires Concerning Human Understanding* (1748). "I flatter myself," Hume triumphantly proclaimed, "that I have discovered an argument . . . which, if just, will, with the wise and learned, be an everlasting check to all kinds of superstitious delusion, and consequently, will be useful as long as the world endures."[12] His everlasting check on superstition begins with a circular argument that because miracles can't happen, a reasonable person should not even listen to reports of them. Hume taught that though the normal job of a historian was to listen to the testimony that comes down to us from the past, there is a point at which you can close your ears. Hume knew that historical testimony can get wild, so he came up with a way to domesticate the wildness, a way to make history a zoo rather than allow it to be a jungle. He has been tremendously influential in the discipline of human history over the last two hundred and fifty years, not because his ideas are strong, but because his ideas are useful. Get rid of "superstitious delusions," and the discipline of history can be turned from a safari into a form of home economics.

Hume's domestication of history is seductively simple. Instead of following the tradition of linking the credibility of hard-to-believe testimony to the credibility of the testifier, Hume recommended disregarding the testifier and focusing only on the testimony. This effectively removed the persuasive power from hard-to-believe testimony. Miracles need the credibility of an eyewitness in order to have persuasive power. Hume cut the testimony away from testifier.[13]

---

12. Hume, *Enquires*, X.i.86.
13. See Kennedy, "Miracles in the Dock," 26:7–22.

Essentially, Hume adopted the modeling technique that Darwin later used and is best seen in your dashboard GPS. Hume recommends gathering testimony from the past and every region to create a general model of what humans generally experience. Using this mass of information, one should generalize standards of common experience. Now if anyone reports a miracle, the alleged event can't be true because it does not conform to the generalized standards of common experience. (Of course, Hume had already refused to allow that any reports of miracles could be used even to generalize common experience.) It's tricky. Its logic is circular. But it works to weed out awkward, quirky information. It is as if a domineering GPS unit created a sphere to serve as an abstraction for the earth, then insisted that the earth can't have wobbling poles and flattening in the upper latitudes because the sphere in the GPS shows it can't be true. Given a useful and trustworthy GPS, don't listen to even a scientist who might tell you something different than what the GPS allows for.

The circularity of this argument has been noted ever since Hume first proposed it, but Hume was a good writer and said what a lot of people wanted to hear.[14] Miracles are impossible so miracle reports can't be true. Don't even listen to reports of them.

Also embedded in Hume's essay is the awkward "rule of logic," most often called "Balancing Likelihoods."[15] By combining math and logic in an odd way, Hume offers another reason why historians should avoid thinking about miracles. Balancing Likelihoods is a beguiling notion that seems reasonable on the surface but is slippery and not necessarily sensible. Balancing Likelihoods has many names but is probably best stated by David Hackett Fischer, in his *Historians' Fallacies: Toward a Logic of Historical Thought*, as "the rule of probability:"

> [A]ll inferences from empirical evidence are probabilistic. It is not, therefore, sufficient to demonstrate merely that A was possibly the case. A historian must determine, as best he can, the probability of A in relation to the probability of alternatives. In the same fashion he cannot disprove A by demonstrating that not-A was possible,

---

14. On the long-running philosophical debates about Hume, see two recent books and their bibliographies: Levine, *Hume and the Problem of Miracles*, and Beckwith, *David Hume's Argument Against Miracles*.

15. Much of what follows is taken from Kennedy, "Faith and History: A Better Understanding of Balancing Likelihoods."

but only by demonstrating that not-A was more probable than A. This is the rule of probability.[16]

Whether called Balancing Likelihoods or the Rule of Probability, this strategy of logic was developed in the eighteenth century by probability theorists who wanted to make the disciplines of history and jurisprudence more mathematically sophisticated. Balancing Likelihoods, in the way described by Fischer, is not used by historians in any normal practice. It is more an idea that never gets used except to avoid reports of miracles. Mathematicians, ever since the eighteenth century, have criticized the applicability of mathematical probability to jurisprudence and history; however, here again, it gives historians a reason not to listen.

Probabilistic logic had been advancing rapidly in the seventeenth century, and there were many attempts to apply quantities to qualities, especially in Christian apologetics and jurisprudence. "Pascal's Wager," the most famous mathematical apologetic from the seventeenth century, equated eternal salvation with mathematical infinity and then applied it to a gambling formula.[17] Antoine Arnauld, in *The Port-Royal Logic* (1662), and John Locke, in his *Essay Concerning Human Understanding* (1690) and *Discourse on Miracles* (1706), carried probabilistic math and logic into the handling of reported miracles. A half-century later, Hume reacted against Arnauld and Locke's teachings that miracles could be handled reasonably.[18] Hume insisted that to handle a reported miracle, a historian had to create two separate ratios, pro and con, for believability. The ratios were then to be weighed against each other. This is Fischer's "rule of probability" quoted above. In the language of Hume's era, this was proclaimed as the "calculus of good sense."

Lorraine Daston, in *Classical Probability in the Enlightenment* (1988), offers an excellent study of Hume and the many eighteenth-century mathematicians who wanted to help bring rigorous quantitative thinking to what today would be called the humanities. Daston writes that by the 1840s, mathematicians realized that "the 'calculus of good sense' had be-

---

16. Fischer, *Historians' Fallacies*, 63.

17. For more on this see Kennedy, "The Application of Mathematics to Christian Apologetics in Pascal's *Pensées* and Arnauld's *The Port-Royal Logic*."

18. The literature on Locke's and Hume's views on miracles is extensive; however, a good place to begin is Burns, *Great Debate on Miracles*.

come antithetical to good sense," and that today most of what these early probabilists were trying to do is considered "patently absurd."[19]

In 1901, one of America's preeminent philosopher-mathematician-logicians, Charles Sanders Peirce, wrote three essays attacking the way historians had adopted Hume's bad logic: "A Preliminary Chapter, Toward an Examination of Hume's Argument Against Miracles, in its Logic and in its History," "Hume's Arguments Against Miracles, and the Idea of Natural Law," and "On the Logic of Drawing History from Ancient Documents especially from Testimonies."[20] Peirce showed that historians are in error when they talk of judging testimony by balancing probabilities because "in a scientific sense, there are no 'probabilities' to be judged."[21] Probability, Peirce wrote, "is the ratio of the frequency of occurrence of a specific event to a generic event." A testimony "is neither a specific event, nor a generic event, but an individual event."[22] Peirce further pointed out that what people were justifying by claiming Balancing Likelihoods was really simply relating "what they prefer to do" to what they don't prefer.[23] "Likelihood is merely a reflection of our preconceived ideas."[24]

Historians like me who want to teach about the Jesus of history have to emphasize commonsense traditions of doing history against the mental world of philosophers such as Collingwood and Hume. That mental world is often criticized by our leading historians. We generally assert the value of practical reason and pragmatic wisdom against philosophical theorists. Dealing wisely with reports of events verging on the incredible is just part of the normal job of being grounded in the social study of our complex human past.

It is reasonable to look to the Bible for history. The Bible is a complex collection of ancient books, many of which were written to tell us information

19. Daston, *Classical Probability*, xviii, xiii. See also Hacking, *Emergence of Probability*, and Kline, *Mathematics*.

20. Page numbers I give come from the only complete modern printing of these works: Peirce, *Historical Perspectives on Peirce's Logic of Science*, ed. Eisele. The best study of Peirce on this subject is Merrill's "Hume's 'Of Miracles,' Peirce, and the Balancing of Likelihoods;" see also Ayers, "C. S. Peirce On Miracles."

21. Peirce, *Historical Perspectives*, 911.

22. Ibid., 911.

23. Ibid., 712.

24. Ibid., 910.

about deep roots of nations, movements of peoples, territorial skirmishes, and the motives of important individuals. Moses is traditionally the first great writer of history in the Bible. God directed him to build an ark, a box, to carry around the "testimonies," the documents of their society. Genesis is a collection of deep oral histories that Moses might have written down and saved in the ark. The New Testament and the consensus of Christian tradition do not demand any one interpretation as to who authored Genesis or how the history in it fits with later notions of history.

I see historical intentions in the Old Testament becoming more clear about a thousand years after Moses, when the Jews freely shared libraries and archives with Iraqis, Iranians, and Egyptians of the Persian Empire. Ezra is a good example of a wholly different concern for history developing in the Persian Empire. The book of Ezra is a historically convoluted and lawyerly argument for a public policy that ends with Ezra being named a Persian bureaucrat. I have my students memorize Ezra 5:17: "Let a search be made of the royal archives." The book of Esther declares its intention to be the historical background for a holiday and names Mordecai as the instigator of writing down the history. The book was probably heavily edited, because it reads like a story to be told around the family dinner table.

Ezra and Esther were probably initially written in the same era that Herodotus was developing Greek history. Jewish/Persian historical methods in narrow books are not like Herodotus' grand compilation of *Histories*. Ezra uses history for public policy. Esther uses history to inspire loyalty and appreciation. Neither is written as an investigation. Neither tells us the range of sources or alternative conclusions in the way Herodotus does. By modern academic standards, Herodotus is clearly the father of a discipline of history, not the writers of biblical history.

But then, Herodotus's *Histories*, like the Bible, has long been accused of being full of lies. Ancient history, whether biblical or Greek, is weak stuff and is vulnerable to cynics, skeptics, and over-thinking dogmatists. Aristotle, Augustine, and long academic tradition teach that the persuasiveness of history relies on a willingness to believe, a willingness to listen, and a willingness to assent to what we learn from other people. *Faith* is a term in Aristotelian logic for the type of knowledge accorded to history. History lies vulnerable to Dave and me too. We want to teach ancient history and try to do our best with the information we have. But we probably get more things wrong than right. What is amazing is that Jesus humbled himself not only by being incarnated in the weakness of flesh, but also that he incarnated knowledge of himself into the weakness of ancient historical writing, writings so easily scoffed at, so easily misunderstood, so easily dismissed as lies.

What makes ancient history especially weak is the few and disparate bits of information available to us. Mere teachers, like Dave and I, and the big name scholars of ancient human history all have to do what is called "harmonizing." We are lucky to have any information at all about most events in the ancient world. Often we only have one source for something. Happily, we sometimes get multiple sources. Sometimes we have a combination of archeology and history complete with inscriptions on stone and written accounts. Whatever we have, it rarely fits together easily. There are usually big gaps and contradictions. We try to harmonize what we have so that we have a history that makes some sense. Harmonizing is full of dangers and pitfalls, but it is the vocation of a historian, whether teaching a class or writing a book.

Dave and Matt moved higher up, picking their way between and over large boulders. Steve, smaller, had a tougher time making his way. I hung back with him. There was no trail at this point. We spread out as we each tried to pick our own way up.

Historians have to think over and over again about how we know things and how strong we know things. One of the greatest moments in ancient history is the fall of Babylon to the Persian armies of Cyrus. Every teenager going to school throughout the world is supposed to learn about it. Our sources are surprisingly strong for such an event. We have diverse accounts of the event that even name individuals within the action. We also have the city's ruins and many accounts of ancient Babylon in general. On the other hand, we have to do some extreme harmonizing to make sense of the story of Persia's conquest—including making a necessary decision whether to tell or to jettison the role of a woman who may be the most important actor in the event.

Five centuries before Jesus, Babylon was the greatest, most impressive city in the world, sitting in a narrow fertile plain between the Tigris and Euphrates Rivers in what is now Iraq. Every world history textbook has a section on the fall of Babylon to the Persian Empire. Knowledge of this event comes from three written sources: the Old Testament, Herodotus, and a collection of short inscriptions.[25] None of the sources tell us much, and only Herodotus is directly interested in the end of Babylon's independence.

D. J. Wiseman offers a standard, authoritative account of the event in the massive *Cambridge Ancient History*. As Wiseman describes the story, the main Babylonian characters are Nebachadrezzar II, who rebuilt and expanded the city into a wonder of the ancient world; Nebachadrezzar's successor, Nabonidus, who absented himself from direct rule of the city and kingdom for religious reasons; and Nabonidus' son Belshazzar, who was delegated the duty of ruling the city. Nebachadrezzar is the name from Babylonian inscriptions, another name for the Bible's Nebuchadnezzar. Nebachadrezzar's reputation as a builder of the grand city is something Wiseman draws from the Bible. With this reputation and archeological remains, Wiseman views Nebachadrezzar as builder of the famous gardens, which are known from later sources.

Of the Persians, Wiseman tells how Cyrus had united the Iranian peoples and conquered much of what is now Turkey and the upper Tigris and Euphrates. Cyrus' army then came south and took Babylon with great speed, without much fight. Nebachadrezzar had already died. Nabonidus surrendered. Belshazzar died during the initial attack. When Cyrus arrived after the battle, he spared the life of Nabonidus, restored order, established official religious toleration, and soon went on to other conquests. While in Babylon, Cyrus gave his blessing and support to Babylonian Jews who desired to rebuild Jerusalem and reinvigorate their culture.

To tell this story smoothly requires much harmonizing of contradictory information. Herodotus contains a royal father and son, but both are named Labynetus (I.188). The book of Daniel has no mention of Nabonidus or Cyrus and instead focuses on Belshazzar and Darius who, Wiseman figures, must have been the two in the actual urban battle. Darius was the on-site military commander and Belshazzar the on-site leader responsible for defending the city. There is no evidence that Cyrus and Nabonidus were at the actual conquest of the city, so the Bible's emphasis on Darius and Balshazzar fits in the gap. Both Daniel and Herodotus tell

---

25. See Evans, "Individuals in Herodotus," and Waters, "Importance of Individuals."

stories of Darius, not Cyrus, ruling the city after the conquest. Nabonidus is only known from appearances in Babylonian records.

All in all, Wiseman offers a reasonable harmonization of who was who and where they were in the conquest of the city. This is what ancient historians do to make sense of the sources. Wiseman is conservative, does not stick his neck out, and uses most everything available to reconstruct the story.

Ancient historians, however, are always debating the reliability of sources and the correct level of harmonization. Many modern historians want to avoid using the Bible. Some modern historians think Herodotus is unreliable. On the other hand, all historians know they can't throw out all their sources. We have to draw a line of belief somewhere. Harmonization is dangerous but necessary.[26] As for me, I think it interesting to press the Babylon story a little further, to include what many historians have thought highly improbable: the story of a dynamic female in the mix of this great event.

Herodotus focuses his own account of the event around a queen named Nitocris. He describes her as wife and mother in relation to the king and prince, both named Labynetus. In Herodotus, the king and his son are inexplicably out of the picture. In the long months leading up to the conquest, no men lead Babylon's defense against the Persians. Queen Nitocris predicts the coming danger and directs the construction of a moat around the city and various other water defenses involving altering the course of the Euphrates River. Nitocris is said to be a Median princess, but her name is Egyptian. Herodotus, sixty or so years after the event, apparently heard the story of an imported political wife who dynamically took charge during a power vacuum in the midst of a crisis. The exploits of an extraordinary woman, whose name he probably got wrong, was the best story he heard when he asked about the conquest of the city.

D. J. Wiseman, in the *Cambridge Ancient History*, weaves the story of the conquest of Babylon by extensive harmonization of the written sources available, but he makes no attempt to harmonize Nitocris into

---

26. For another example of harmonizing the Bible with Herodotus and Persian sources, see Yamauchi's excellent *Persia and the Bible*. Recent arguments for the general trustworthiness of Herodotus include *Historian's Craft in the Age of Herodotus*, ed. Luraghi; and Romm, *Herodotus*. The strongest argument against trusting Herodotus for history and instead dismissing all his references to sources as a type of fiction is Fehling, *Herodotus and His "Sources."*

the story. In his book *Nebachadrezzar and Babylon*, he notes the archeological evidence for the water defenses but dismisses without explanation the existence of Nitocris as "legendary."[27] Wiseman, drawing an inference from Hebrew scriptures, has king Nebachadrezzar responsible for *all* the construction work in and around Babylon. Following Wiseman's lead, Carolyn Dewald, in her notes to the *Oxford World's Classics* edition of Herodotus, writes that "Nitocris does not seem to have existed ... but may be H's misunderstanding of the role played by Nebachadrezzar."[28] Dewald discounts Herodotus' report that it was Nitocris who was an active builder in Babylon. Amélie Kuhrt dismisses the harmonization project and is willing to dismiss the history of Nitocris. In *Civilizations of the Ancient Near East*, Kuhrt writes that "trying to unravel the Herodotean account and to match historically attested Mesopotamian royal figures with the queens are impossible, and perhaps also misconceived."[29]

Giving up on Nitocris in the narrative of Babylon's conquest has become the standard way of handling Herodotus' account of her. A foreign-born queen in the most wondrous city of the ancient world, foreseeing the threat from the leader of the people of her birth, chooses to lead her adopted people in the construction of defensive water works during a period when the men who surround her are unable to act. It is a great moment in history. It's a great story. But the evidence is weak, the story awkward (Where was the king?), and Herodotus leaves a lot of holes unfilled. The story is too complex. Harmonization is indeed "impossible, and perhaps also misconceived."

The trouble with abandoning the story of Nitocris is that there is no version of the story that does *not* require extensive harmonizing of awkward and dubious information. The story is full of holes filled by speculations no matter how it is told. Any version of the story a historian wants to tell will require harmonizing bits and pieces of information and giving awkward sources the "benefit of the doubt." How the story of Babylon's conquest is told is a slippery question that is usually more a matter of a historian's gut feelings than consistent method. In the culture of universities, our gut feeling is supposed to be counseled to follow the natural science principle loosely called Ockham's Razor. When in doubt,

27. Wiseman, *Nebachadrezzar and Babylon*, 57.
28. Herodotus, *Histories*, 612.
29. Kuhrt, "Ancient Near East," I, 59–60; see also Beaulieu, "King Nabonidus," II, 969–79.

a historian should go with the simpler story. However, in ancient history, especially if you want to tell of the actions of any individuals, especially individual women, even the simplest stories are a stretch.[30] The question becomes how far does one stretch, how far does one harmonize, and is there warrant for such stretching and harmonizing?

There is warrant to harmonize Nitocris into the standard story. Daniel chapter four tells an odd story of Nebuchadnezzar's mental breakdown to the point where he apparently thought himself an animal. Wiseman does not discount the possibility and notes awkward gaps in the Babylonian Chronicles during the years leading up to the conquest.[31] Daniel has Nebuchadnezzar eating grass, growing his hair and nails, and losing his sanity for what seems to have been a significant length of time. Babylonian sources have Nabonidus unconcerned with civic duties and more interested in religious rites performed in the desert. Herodotus reports no moves by the king or his son to defend the city. A power vacuum is indicated in the three major sources, and presumably a farsighted queen could have stepped into a position of leadership.

Not only does the story of Nitocris fit an indicated situation, it also does not contradict any information given in other sources. There is no other source that says someone else first saw the danger of the rising Persians and then led the construction of the water defenses that we know existed. Nebachadrezzar is in several places named as a great builder and is proud of his work, but nowhere is it claimed that he built what Herodotus accords to Nitocris. Herodotus does not claim Nitocris called for the construction of the walls, the palace, or the Hanging Gardens. (Berossus, writer of a third century BC history of Babylon, has Nitocris responsible for the Hanging Gardens.)[32] Keeping Nitocris in the construction story does no violence to any source, while taking her out does do violence to one of the major sources.

---

30. There are forms of history relatively unconcerned with individuals. Women's history, as a field, is generally unconcerned with inquiry into an ancient queen such as Nitocris. See Pomeroy, *Women's History*; Archer, et.al., *Women in Ancient Societies*; and Kuhrt, "Non-Royal Women." Note also that in Bahrani's *Women of Babylon*, 176, Nitocris is not mentioned but another queen named by Herodotus, Samaris, is analyzed for perceptions of her role in the construction of Babylon.

31. Wiseman, *Nebachadrezzar*, 105–7.

32. See Wiseman, "Palace and Temple Gardens," 37–43.

Mount Darwin

All three major sources have an influential queen-figure. Hebrew scriptures echo Herodotus' statement that an intelligent queen saw the danger coming. In Daniel chapter five, an unnamed queen is crucial to the scene when "the writing on the wall" is interpreted and the coming of the Persians is prophesied. A "queen" in such an instance can be a mother, a wife, a grandmother, or any other woman in the palace of that vague rank. In Babylonian sources there is Adad-guppi, Nabonidus' mother, who, like Nitocris in Herodotus, was a captive Median girl married into Babylonian royalty to solidify a political alliance. Adad-guppi became a queen in a polygamous royal household but was special enough for Nabonidus to erect a funerary stele with an account of her religious life.[33]

Herodotus, Daniel, and the stele of Adad-guppi all point to an extraordinary woman of queen rank active in the last days of independent Babylon. If we are to tell the story of the last days at all, we have to do some creative harmonizing. Why not add the queen into the harmony? Wiseman, in the *Cambridge Ancient History*, stretches even to make sense between the known size of Babylon and Aristotle's wild statement that it took three days for information of the Persian attack to spread from one side of the city to the other. To add Herodotus' story of a dynamic queen into this standard narrative of events is a stretch, but it has warrant. Amélie Kuhrt may be right to say it is impossible to match precisely the various attestations of Mesopotamian queens; much in ancient history is not precise. Is it really "misconceived" to attempt harmonizing reports of a queen foreseeing a foreign threat while the male leaders dithered in the last days of independent Babylon?

This is the kind of work ancient historians do behind the scenes of general education textbooks. These are the kinds of questions they face. Big leaps with little support are on every page of history textbooks. Harmonizing of disparate, sometimes contradictory, evidence is standard. Crucial decisions (Do we mention the woman or not?) are made out of feelings of tension about the extent to which stretching is warranted.

"Come to history as a doubter," Richard Marius advises in a historical methods manual. "Skepticism is one of the historian's finest qualities. Historians don't trust their sources.... Nothing is quite so destructive to a historian's reputation as to present conclusions that prove gullibility."[34]

---

33. Dillery gives a short bibliography of attempts to harmonize Nitocris and Adad-guppi in footnote #6 of "Darius and the Tomb of Nitocris (Hdt. I.187)," 31.

34. Marius, *Short Guide*, 67, 48.

But Marius is wrong. In practice, historians have to trust more than doubt. In practice, historians, especially ancient historians, can't rely on doubting. Historians have to be close listeners, discerning listeners, wise listeners, who sometimes have to make harmonies and stretch for belief.

Dave once led me on a road-trip study of the twelfth- and thirteenth-century Indians of the Southwest. Dave, at the time, was student president of our Phi Alpha Theta history honor society. Cliff dwellings came up in class, and Dave organized a road trip to see as many Mogollon, Hohokam, and Anasazi ruins as can be done in an October four-day weekend.

Elbows in the breeze, my boys in the way back, a car-full of students following, we drove east from San Diego to Casa Grande and Montezuma's Castle near Phoenix. Approaching Mesa Verde we hit snow. Our last night, we camped at Canyon de Chelly, east of Flagstaff. At every site, we were frustrated by the silence of the ruins. We could imagine life in these impressive buildings and speculate on why they were built and abandoned. However, we learned no specific names, nothing of political innovations, next to nothing about major events. Unrelenting mystery engulfed every site.

The cliff dwellings are, in many ways, as impressive as the ruins of Athens and Corinth, but we know so much more about genius of the latter's citizens. The Greeks tell us about themselves, their leaders, the heroes, their gods, their acts. We listen and learn. In the Southwest we knew we were in the presence of genius, but there we could only listen to a frustrating silence.

The life of Jesus is noisy. A cacophony of information reaches through two thousand years to communicate with us. In the Bible alone we have four organized biographical sketches, Luke's history of the first decades after Jesus, and a bunch of letters. Intersecting Jesus and the New Testament is an amazing amount of Roman literature dealing with Syria and Palestine, which were important and unruly parts of the empire. An important Jewish/Greek historian, Josephus, wrote books about Israel that contribute to our knowledge of Jesus' time. From the Bible and Josephus, historians have much more information about Jesus and the social and political issues of Jerusalem than any person or place in Europe at the same time.

Mount Darwin

On top of all of the noise of good information in the Bible and Josephus, a large library of books, called the "Dead Sea Scrolls," were discovered in the middle of the twentieth century. We have much more information about Jesus to fight about than we have for almost any other person you read about in ancient history. Our sources are strong and diverse. We have multiple testimonies from highly credible sources, sources willing to live and die by the truth of their testimony.

Ironically, we have so much information that is essentially consistent and reliable, that we historians nitpick fights about all sorts of little things. Historians are frustrated when they don't have information, but they become hypercritical when they have lots of information. We harmonize, then criticize, then revise, then harmonize again. We chase our tails. Many are so overwhelmed by so much information that they turn their back on the information. They declare that we can't expect to ever know the real "historical" Jesus.

There is some truth in what they say. The discipline of history is a blunt instrument—in the university pocketknife, we are the awkward can-opener tool. Historians don't have the knife-blade precision of controlled, repeatable experiments or the screwdriver leverage of geometrical demonstrations. By high standards of scientific precision or by high standards of philosophy, we don't "know" historical people—be they Jesus or Caesar Augustus—really. However, by the practical standards of history, we know about Jesus as much, probably more, than we know about most ancient people, even Caesar Augustus.

Those who proclaim that we can't know the "historical" Jesus are usually folks who don't want to listen to the noise of so many good sources. Instead of listening to hear about Jesus, they want to create a Jesus. They want to create a more modern Jesus, a rational Jesus.

Giving up on the historical—traditional—Jesus is the first step to giving up on a Christianity strong enough to withstand any overblown Darwinian claims. Darwinism's greatest threat to Christianity depends on the bait-and-switch of substituting a rationalized Jesus for the biblical Jesus. When we get to the top of Mount Darwin, we will be able to see Mount Fiske to the south. John Fiske can remind us of the danger in substituting a rational Jesus for the real one reported in history.

John Fiske was a modern-minded young man from the start. He was born in Middletown, Connecticut in 1842 with the name Edmund Fisk Green. In college he changed his name to John Fisk, and then when he became an author he added an "e" to the end. Before leaving home for college, his concerned grandmother asked after his religious belief:

> In her sore perplexity, grandma asked whether I believed in the Bible, meaning whether I believed everything in it; of course I said no. I couldn't lie even to save her feelings. She felt bad about it. She asked me if I didn't believe Christ was God, and of course, again I had to say no. How can a man have two natures without having two medulla oblongatas? A double ego, a double center of innervation is something to which I cannot yet subscribe.[35]

Fiske was a smart kid wanting to be on the intellectual cutting edge. In his junior year at Harvard, he was caught reading Auguste Compte in chapel. Much like young Solomons, Fiske wanted to be a writer. Some writers become writers because they study a discipline; writing becomes the means of communicating the fruit of their study. Fiske was the kind of writer who wants to write because his mind bubbled with all sorts of thoughts about religion, science, politics, and people. Before working at a university, he wrote on university reform. Eventually, as a university librarian, he wrote on religion and history. When he got famous enough, he quit being a librarian to become a traveling intellectual, publishing his lectures and reviews as they accumulated.

Like many nineteenth-century historians, Fiske wrote history largely to prove that modern people are smarter than ancient people. Such historians don't love history for a larger sense of community and experience; they find it self-justifying and gratifyingly isolating. History, for them, is the story of progress. The historian becomes magisterial and dispenses praise and blame, honor and pity at will. Listen to Fiske's magisterial tone when talking about the past as childlike:

> No religious creed that man has ever devised can be made to harmonize in all its features with modern knowledge. All such creeds were constructed with reference to theories of the universe which are now utterly and hopelessly discarded. How, then, it is asked, amid the general wreck of old beliefs, can we hope that the religious attitude in which from time immemorial we have been wont to contemplate the universe can any longer be maintained? Is not the belief in God perhaps a dream of the childhood of our race, like the belief in elves and bogarts which once were no less

---

35. Quoted in Winston, *John Fiske*, 20.

universal? and is not modern science fast destroying the one as it has already destroyed the other?[36]

God, elves, and the bogeyman versus modern science. The reader is shamed into joining the writer's triumphal modernity. Biblical accounts of Jesus, of course, must be rationalized so as to fit our adult/modern minds. Many biblical reports of events and statements have to be jettisoned so that the "real" Jesus can be found.

In a review article entitled "The Jesus of History" (1870), Fiske declared that we have "but few facts resting upon trustworthy evidence" for Jesus.[37] The words of Jesus are "preserved by hearsay tradition through the generation immediately succeeding his death," and that generation cannot be trusted to distinguish the "authentic utterances of the great teacher from the later interpolations suggested by the dogmatic necessities of the narrators." The early church was duped into a history of Jesus by its own "uncritical spirit," its own lack of a rational historical method that could have preserved a genuine history.[38] Fiske then offered a quick survey of an appropriate "method of inquiry which, in the hands of the so-called Tübingen School, has led to such striking and valuable conclusions concerning the age and character of all the New Testament literature."[39] Fiske particularly praises David Friedrich Strauss's *The Life of Jesus Critically Examined* (1835–36) and praises early nineteenth-century German biblical scholarship.[40] This new German scholarship supported the French tradition evident in the book that Fiske was reviewing: an anonymous work published in 1869 derived from the internationally popular French *Life of Jesus* written by J. D. Renan in 1863.

Renan's book was reprinted and translated many times. In it, Renan declared his desire to get at a genuine history of Jesus. He criticized his German predecessors for their overemphasis on philosophy and wrote in a simplified critical spirit that discarded impossibilities and discounted the given narratives while offering conjectures about what really happened and what really was said. Of course, there was no actual historical resurrection. Renan's Jesus was the Son of God because he taught that true worship is

36. Winston, *John Fiske*, 81–82.
37. Fiske, "Jesus of History," 66–67.
38. Ibid., 69.
39. Ibid., 74.
40. Ibid., 76.

not tied to earthly places and rituals. Given the popularity of his book, we can assume that Renan struck a deep chord in lots of people who wanted a vaguely rational Jesus who was anti-clerical and might even be a liberal Protestant. Renan's Jesus was a guy who would fit well in a faculty meeting. It was the disciples who embarrass us with pseudo-historical stories of the transfiguration, walking on water, and the resurrection.

Fiske supported books that supported the search for the rational Jesus. The Bible obfuscates more than illuminates. To find the truth, the scholar must go behind what is reported in the Bible to find the bits and pieces of the "true" Jesus that poke from underneath. This "true" Jesus unearthed by modern scholarship is the Jesus of the bait and switch. Once a rational Jesus is established, then a rational guy like Fiske can knock him down. The abstraction of Jesus can't win against the stronger abstractions of natural history. My GPS is bigger than your GPS.

This is the central problem with the common claim of scientists. Stephen Gould, in *Rocks of Ages: Science and Religion in the Fullness of Life* (1999), insisted that science is about facts, experimental results, and natural reality, while Christianity is about values, ethics, and things taught in literature classes. Christianity can't breathe in the realm of abstractions. If Christianity is about values, then I would rather be Confucian. Christianity has to be about facts, facts about a teacher who not only messed with the laws of nature, but rose from the dead, confirming his own claims, reported to us in ancient history.

At about 11,400 feet, we rounded the shoulder of a ridge and walked into a frozen meadow filled with iced-over streams trickling among large tufts of dormant grass made brittle by the cold. Another 500 feet above us was Blue Heaven Lake. Mount Darwin dominated the western skyline. We were moving slower than I had hoped, but now our goal was in plain sight, calling us onward. The sun was bright, the sky blue, and the climb was just a matter of scrambling up, around, and over steep piles of rocks. Here in the meadow, Dave pumped our water bottles full for our ascent. Matt and Steve giggled as they tentatively inched out onto small pools, testing the ice.

Charles Darwin was more than interested in nature. He truly loved it. In *The Voyage of the Beagle*, he is a kid in a candy store. He was twenty-two years old when the *Beagle* reached the coast of Brazil after leaving England:

> The day was passed delightfully. Delight itself, however, is a weak term to express the feelings of a naturalist who, for the first time, has wandered by himself in a Brazilian forest. The elegance of the grasses, the novelty of the parasitical plants, the beauty of the flowers, the glossy green of the foliage, but above all the general luxuriance of the vegetation, filled me with admiration. A most paradoxical mixture of sound and silence pervades the shady parts of the wood. The noise from the insects is so loud, that it may be heard even in a vessel anchored several hundred yards from the shore; yet within the recesses of the forest a universal silence appears to reign. To a person fond of natural history, such a day as this brings with it a deeper pleasure than he can ever hope to experience again.[41]

You have to love a guy who loves natural history that much.

Natural history and human history overlap in the creation of calendars. The Western standard calendar uses the birth of Jesus for measuring years backwards and forwards, but we don't know Jesus' exact birth, death, or ascension dates. Ancient history has a lot of soft dates. The hard dates we have usually come from matters we can figure out from reported astronomical events. Our strongest calendar dates for events in the ancient past are found by the GPS-style modeling of natural history.

The New Testament reports that Jesus was born when a star appeared during the reign of Caesar Augustus (27 BC to AD 14). We are now pretty sure that Jesus was born between 4 and 6 BC. To say that Christ was born 4 to 6 years "Before Christ" is a bit awkward. It is probably better intellectually to say Jesus was born 4 to 6 years "Before the Common Era" (BCE). The chronology of Jesus' birth that created our modern calendar was stabilized in the sixth century by monks comparing all the ancient literature and astronomical calculations they could get hold of. What is amazing is not that they missed the right year, but that they were so close!

Jesus was born, as pieced together from the gospels, when Augustus was emperor, Herod was a king, Quirinius was governor of Syria, and a census was decreed. All four of these are squishy. Augustus ruled a long

---

41. Darwin, *Voyage of the Beagle*, 13–14.

time. The terms "governor" and "Syria" are vague, because "governor" is a generic term like "queen," and Syria had both a specific and generic designation in geography. As for censuses, we know of some specific census decrees, such as one in 8 BC. Overall, it is surprising how little we know about bureaucratic matters in the Roman Empire.

We know more about Herod than most government officials because of the historian Josephus. Herod, we are told, died shortly after an eclipse of the moon visible from Jericho, but before the subsequent Passover. This is a rare bit of specific information to have reported to us. Given the regularity of Passovers and that natural history can calculate eclipses, Herod probably died in late March or early April of 4 BC.

The astronomical event for dating the birth of Jesus is the star that the wise men followed. Astrophysicist Mark Kidger has written the most recent book on the subject: *The Star of Bethlehem: An Astronomer's View* (1999). Kidger starts his inquiry at the right place. He assumes there is something historically true going on in the gospel description of a star. He then assumes that the star was not a one-time miracle event, but rather something understandable using "sound science, logic, and educated guesswork." He then takes the historical account in the gospels as reliable until proven otherwise. He takes the death date of Herod discussed above as accurate and combines it with a reasonable account of a star over Bethlehem.[42]

Kidger has to cross back and forth between ancient history, astronomy, and even ancient Chinese astronomy to come to a range of options as to what would lead astronomer-magi from Mesopotamia toward Judea. What Kidger settles on are three astronomical events beginning in 7 BC that were treated as signs with a fourth event, a nova, in March of 5 BC.

Overlapping natural history and human history is often productive. Ideally, the historical reliability of ancient information is best when we have multiple texts in general agreement about people, places, and events; archeology offers physical support; and natural history gives us an exact date. We Christians have pretty strong history. The reliability is amazingly high when compared with what we know about most Roman emperors, senators, and generals.

Craig Blomberg's *The Historical Reliability of the Gospels* (1987) is a good overview of what we can piece together now. Blomberg is right to emphasize the "reliability" of the New Testament historical narratives as a first

---

42. Kidger, *Star of Bethlehem*, ix–x.

step toward fuller understanding of the whole Bible and the Holy Spirit's role in the Bible's authority. In the fullness of Christianity and the Church, the Bible is much more than just reliable; however, at a university it is best to accept the limited language of historical reliability. A university is not a church. In terms of goals and methods, universities are much smaller.

Jesus humbled himself to become part of Roman historical literature. The Roman standards for that literature were low. Absolute certainty was not expected. What was expected was an author's desire to tell the factual truth to the best of an author's ability, especially if the author was not an eyewitness and had to rely on oral and written reports. The gospels fit into a flexible genre of Roman historical literature called *bios*, or short "lives."[43] Publius Terentius Varro apparently wrote the first such "life of" around 44 BC. The most famous collections were written in the first two centuries after Jesus: Plutarch's *Parallel Lives of the Noble Greeks and Romans*, Suetonius' *Lives of the Twelve Caesars*, and Diogenese Laertius' *Lives of the Philosophers*. These collections of short biographical sketches follow patterns from the founding Greek historians, Herodotus and Thucydides, in their conscientious desire to get at the truth of speeches, events, and the role of varied human characters in the decisions that move history.

Christopher Pelling, an ancient historian at Oxford University, has an essay on "Truth and Fiction in Plutarch's *Lives*." Pelling is a conscientious listener-historian. He understands Plutarch's need to shorten speeches, wrestle with chronology, make sense of a person's movements, and give enough political and social context for the reader to have a portrait of the importance of a person's life. The goal is to do all this quickly in one scroll length. In the twentieth century, it became common for critics to treat Plutarch more as a novelist than as a historian. Pelling, however, shows how such criticism does not understand Plutarch's project "to understand what really happened and people as they really behaved."[44] Plutarch was writing history within the acceptable limits of a genre of short sketched lives.

Luke, in his opening paragraphs to Luke and Acts, conscientiously ties himself to the Greek historical tradition of commenting on sources, method, and the purpose for writing. Luke investigates oral and written sources and offers an "orderly account." The goal is a short, reliable, organized overview of the life and teachings of Jesus. Plutarch similarly

---

43. See Burridge, *What Are the Gospels?*
44. Pelling, *Plutarch and History*, 162.

discusses the goal of writing a short sketch life in the opening to his account of Alexander the Great. What is most important in Luke's account is the conscientious admission to the reader that though he is the creator of the books, he is not an eyewitness to Jesus or the earliest history of the church in Jerusalem. The tradition of historical authorship to which he attaches himself is a humble tradition. He offers no overblown authority for himself. On the other hand, he accepts responsibility for the historical reliability of his account.[45] The clearest marks of Greek-style history, ever since Herodotus some four centuries before Jesus, are discussions of sources, claims to authority or credibility, and an implicit request to be believed. At one much debated part of his account of a meeting, Herodotus pleads with his readers to believe him: "There are those in Greece who are not convinced of the authenticity of the speeches that were delivered there, but they did take place."[46]

Thucydides, when explaining his method of writing, notes that he relied much on hearsay from eyewitnesses and implicitly asks for his readers to simply believe that he has applied "the most severe and detailed tests possible" to these reports.[47] Josephus, in his preface to *The Wars of the Jews*, offers a long description of his reliance on hearsay evidence and claims that he has done his best to avoid bias. Tacitus, who was born about twenty-five years after Jesus died, thought that the most important political story of Rome's transition from republic to empire was the story of personal intrigues in Caesar Augustus' family and household. The rise of the empire depends on Augustus' wife Livia's concern that the succession go to her son Tiberius, and Augustus' granddaughter Agrippina's manipulations to bring her son Nero to the throne. Tacitus makes the usual claims to investigating texts, eyewitnesses, and hearsay, but feels obligated to also admit to his readers that he is using rumors that tend to fly around Rome. At one point, when reporting something that seems "fantastic," he cries out: "What I have told, and shall tell, is the truth. Older men heard and recorded it."[48]

Cicero, a few decades before Jesus, in a textbook on being an educated gentleman, wrote that what distinguishes historians is that they are not liars.

---

45. See the extensive discussions of the historical tradition in Bauckham's *Jesus and the Eyewitnesses* and Marincola's *Authority and Tradition*.

46. Herodotus, *Histories*, III.80.

47. Thucydides, *Peloponneisan War*, I.22.

48. Tacitus, *Annals of Imperial Rome*, 246.

Mount Darwin

Cicero declared that it was a great responsibility to be a historian and that the "first law" of the discipline was "that an author must not dare to tell anything but the truth." For Cicero and Roman education in general, the historian is rooted in reported facts, actual chronology, real geography. The historian is not a novelist, is not even a public-policy advocate. The historian is a truth-teller whose speech is plain and purpose clear.[49]

Cicero states the Roman ideal. It is still the ideal. Historians investigate reports and plead with their students and readers to believe them. In modern books, we use footnotes that challenge readers implicitly: "If you don't believe me, go look it up for yourself." At bottom, all modern ancient historians must cry out alongside Herodotus, Thucydides, Luke, Josephus, and Tacitus: "Believe me! I am telling you the best I can give about the past."

Setting aside the question of inerrancy or inspiration by the Holy Spirit—two teachings that are very hard to work with in the university—we have the simpler, more traditional Greek notion of historical reliability. The gospels were written as missionary literature to tell good historical news to people embedded in Greek culture. The biographical sketches of Jesus were written in Greek to people who thought in Greek ways. Even the gospels written with an emphasis on Jewish prophesy were written in Greek for the Jews living throughout the Greek-speaking half of the Roman Empire. If the gospel writers had been interested in exact preservation of Jesus' teachings, they would have written in the language Jesus used. The gospels were written to have legs. The goal was to write something short, well-organized, and reliable in the Roman genre of *bios*, using Greek ways of thinking about historical reliability.

Reading the different historical books in the New Testament, Greek-thinking people would not have been worried about the minor contradictions. The contradictions—such as who went where first at the time of the resurrection or when Jesus actually turned over the temple tables—actually *raise* the authority of the gospels as reliable testimony. Just like police who immediately separate witnesses, nobody expects witnesses to report all the details in the same way. Collusion is suspected if the exact same story is told the same way. Modern historians may still debate a lot about the life of Emperor Nero, but all of them have to face the fact that the three main

---

49. Cicero, *De Oratore*, II.51–64, especially 62–63.

sources of information, Suetonius, Tacitus, and Dio Cassius, did not collude, agreeing on all the essentials, for they do not agree on everything. If the gospels had been exactly alike, their reliability would be diminished.

The diverse incongruities in the five historical books of the New Testament show us that we have four separate authors sharing and not sharing certain sources. The fact that we have five accounts with contradictions shows us that no early bunch of backroom editors crafted our New Testament. If the early church wanted to control the information getting out to the people, they would not have left so many obvious problems and instead would have created one authoritative story. The five historical books of the New Testament are different in many ways but agree on the key points: the resurrection and Jesus' use of that resurrection as part of an offer of salvation to humans. The blatant contradictions actually serve to raise the credibility of their shared accounts of the resurrection. On the other hand, the events and teachings that appear in more than one gospel but in similar structure and wording—for example the transfiguration or walking on water—are actually weaker historically because the similarities indicate multiple authors using one source. Remember, Luke tells us there are written sources he draws from. A reasonable Greek way of working with historical reliability helps strengthen the account of the resurrection. It is in this context of Greek reasonableness that Paul reminds the Corinthians about the many eyewitnesses, more than 500, to the risen Jesus.

The links passing down eyewitness testimony are crucial to the historical reliability of the gospel account of the resurrection. Luke, in a very creative move by the standards of Greek and Roman history writing, set out in the book of Acts to write the history of a movement, especially its bureaucratization and the example of its model missionary. It is an awkward book that sort of fizzles in the end, but the awkwardness increases its historical reliability. If I had to give Luke a grade in one of my classes, I would have to be harsh. The first half is well-organized, but the second half falls apart in personal narrative and over-concern for Roman-Palestinian jurisprudence. Then there is that long conclusion centered on a detailed account of how to handle a ship in a storm. What was he thinking? The book of Acts gives us, by ancient standards, a huge, long account of a ship in a storm, far surpassing the length of Luke's earlier account of Jesus calming a storm or walking on water. If I were his teacher, I would have had to call Luke to my office and tell him to rewrite the last two chapters and resubmit.

However, from the point of view of historical reliability rather than good writing, the awkwardness indicates the immediacy of the first-person narrative. Luke ceases to investigate eyewitnesses and becomes an eyewitness. Maritime historians find the last two chapters of Acts some of the best material available from the ancient world for storm tactics on the Mediterranean.[50] Many modern biblical critics insist that Luke made things up, such as Paul's hassles with the cult of the goddess Artemis in Ephesus. Some say, like some also say of Herodotus' *Histories*, that Acts is more historical novel than history. I am not convinced. Luke's book of Acts isn't crafted well enough. As Cicero intimated, the plainness of history writing allows rough edges that more novelistic history writing would avoid. Xenophon's novelistic history of his heroic retreat from Iraq, to the Black Sea, then back to the Aegean Sea, would have been Luke's model if he was trying to write a travel adventure. What is written in Acts seems consistent with Luke's stated historical purpose: to give an account first of Jesus and the spread of the good news of Jesus that hinges on the resurrection and the "convincing proofs" of multiple eyewitnesses to the resurrection.[51]

As historical knowledge of the resurrection passes from eyewitnesses to hearsay, the crucial links to historical reliability come in the first few centuries. Paul indicates for us that there was conscious gathering, even counting, of eyewitnesses. The multiplicity of eyewitness accounts was an issue for Greek and Roman historical reliability. Another crucial issue was the character of the witnesses. Accounts of persecution and sufferings of eyewitnesses helped establish their character as reporters of truth. In the book of Acts, the truth of the gospel is partly carried by the authority of Stephen and Paul, who are willing to suffer and die for the story. The most important Roman historian to carry on from the book of Acts was a bishop named Eusebius who had been educated in Caesarea a couple centuries after Peter had converted Cornelius there. Eusebius was an extraordinarily prolific and dedicated scholar, and Caesarea was an administrative center with a tradition of education, jurisprudence, and libraries. The eyewitness

---

50. See Casson, *Ancient Mariners*, 211–12; and Smith, "Shipwreck According to St. Luke."

51. Acts 1:3.

traditions of Jesus' life, death, and resurrection were strong in Caesarea. Eusebius was educated in a Christian school there that baptized the Greek curriculum for Christian use. His teacher descended intellectually from a line of dedicated and innovative Christian scholars reaching back to Alexandria in Egypt, the great center of Greek and Roman scholarship. Historians of ancient Rome are still amazed by the breadth and quality of Eusebius' analysis of ancient texts and collation of ancient chronology. He was one of the great scholars in the Roman Empire: a Christian who "regarded the Bible as key to a correct understanding of human history."[52]

Christians who trust the reliability of history in the Bible should take comfort in early Christian scholarship. It is common in our day to hear stories of lackadaisical medieval scribes introducing errors into the Bible; however, there was, in the first five hundred years of Christianity, no collection of books that received higher, more precise, or more comprehensive scholarly protection. Even "errors" such as differences between various versions of texts and contradictions within a given text were protected. The various versions of the Old Testament and copies of Christian writings were preserved and their textual problems studied and discussed. In the first five hundred years, there was no effort by scholars to craft their own Bible. Eusebius and his fellow students of Jewish and Christian writings wanted to collect and study, warts and all, the history that came down to them. Our Bible is strong. It is probably the most scholarly cared-for collection of texts to come to us from the Roman Empire.

Eusebius was the most important of the early Christian scholars who understood that the historical link to the eyewitness tradition needed to be documented. In *The History of the Church*, Eusebius wrote an innovative institutional history that built upon what Luke had started in the book of Acts. Throughout the book, Eusebius used the careful but tentative language of Greek history developed by Herodotus. He tells of his sources and associates them to authorities for reliability. He notes his speculative leaps with phrases such as "it seems" and "it is not improbable" and "this is how I see the matter." In book three, he ties a lot of early history together, including the bishop Polycarp (born probably in 69), "on whom the eyewitnesses and ministers of the Lord had conferred the episcopate."[53] Here "the eyewitnesses" have a special authority in the church. Polycarp,

---

52. Barnes, *Constantine and Eusebius*, 101. On Eusebius as a scholar, see also Grafton and Williams, *Christianity and the Transformation of the Book*.

53. Eusebius, *History of the Church*, 3.36.

Eusebius tells us, "was not only instructed by apostles," but also "conversant with many who had seen the Lord." As bishop, he "taught the things which he had learnt from the apostles, which the Church transmits."[54]

Eusebius searched for the links of eyewitness tradition to his own time three hundred years later. In book five, he goes back to Clement of Alexandria, the founder of his school tradition, who died around 215. He quotes Clement taking notes, "as a tonic for a bad memory," of conversations with old men he found who "preserved the true tradition of the blessed teaching straight from Peter, James, John, and Paul, the holy apostle, son receiving it from father. . . . By the grace of God, they came right down to me, to deposit those ancestral apostolic seeds."[55] Eusebius also quotes Irenaeus, born about 130, on the historical links carrying the gospels into the next generation, mentioning that John's revelations were "not seen a long time back, but almost in my own lifetime."[56]

Luke and Eusebius were historians clearly relying on the Greek tradition of writing reliable history. Eusebius's education can be directly linked through teachers, textbooks, and curriculum to the Aristotelian traditions of history taught in Alexandria, the center of Greek learning. Luke investigated reports from eyewitnesses. Eusebius saw himself picking up where Luke left off. Eusebius writes of the extensive network of bishops, scholars, and martyrs active within churches, schools, and libraries that for a couple of centuries carried Jesus' life and teachings through "peaceful wars," succeeding as "God's commonwealth."[57]

A widespread consensus of people and institutions supported the oral and written testimonies through the first couple hundred years. There was no conspiracy of a small group of people trying to promulgate a narrow view of Jesus. Christianity was broadly supported by trustworthy people and institutions throughout the empire. The Christian scholarly spirit was open and ready to let the stories of Jesus stand up for themselves. The best example of this is Eusebius' commentary on the biography of a first century Pythagorean wise man/holy man/miracle worker from Cappadocia named Apollonius. An antagonist to Christianity named Sossianus Hierocles promoted the long biography of Apollonius as a way

---

54. Ibid., 4.14.
55. Ibid., 5.11.
56. Ibid., 5.8.
57. Ibid., 5.Introduction.

to disparage the Jesus of the gospels. Eusebius's reply is rather lighthearted. He accepts the basic story of Apollonius and allows the possibility that Apollonius could perform miracles, but shows repeatedly that there are problems within the text that diminish its credibility to reasonable people. Eusebius shows the confidence of the church in the midst of pagan culture and pagan history. The gospels of Jesus, the book of Acts, and the letters of Paul were "recognized" by wide consensus as standing in "firm tradition."[58] There was no other Roman holy man or miracle worker whose story had similar power to persuade people.

I have read *The Life of Apollonius* along with Roman "gospels" such as those of Thomas, Judas, and Mary Magdalene.[59] I encourage you to read them. Nothing is more convincing of the wisdom, reliability, and power of the New Testament than reading the writings it competed against. The history preserved in the first two hundred years of Christianity is very strong by the standards of ancient history. The resurrection of Jesus is reported in multiple different accounts. The links between eyewitnesses and the authorities of the next generation were investigated and described. The first two hundred years of the church has many mysteries, but the critical event has an unbroken chain at the center of a widespread network of people and institutions. Conspiracy theorists throughout the ages have tried to promote alternative stories. However, historians such as Luke and Eusebius were careful to give the evidence required by Aristotelian standards to reasonably link the multiple eyewitnesses of high character to the ongoing tradition of hearsay reports in the church, Bible, and creeds.

---

58. Ibid., 3.24–25.

59. Philostratus' *Life of Apollonius of Tyana* is easily available in the Loeb three volume edition that includes Eusebius' *"Reply . . . to the work of Philostratus on Apollonius concerning the comparison between him and Christ handed down by Hierocles."* The Internet is a wonderful treasury of Roman literature for and against Christ.

Mount Darwin

Today only twenty or so people in succession separate us from the eyewitnesses to Jesus' resurrection.[60] Wendell Berry, in his novel *Jayber Crow* (2000), has Jayber, an aging village barber, reminisce:

> History grows shorter. I remember old men who remembered the Civil War. I have in my mind word-of-mouth memories more than a hundred years old. It is only twenty hundred years since the birth of Christ. Fifteen or twenty memories such as mine would reach all the way back to the halo-light in the manger at Bethlehem. So few rememberers could sit down together in a small room.[61]

Our modern schools do much to undermine the closeness of history. Our history textbooks encourage us to think of ourselves as separated from the past. We are taught to assume the past to be a foreign and exotic place. A vast distance is supposed to exist between us and the eyewitnesses to the resurrection. Trusting the reported events in the New Testament is considered a "leap" of faith, something risky, possibly unreasonable. But Jayber Crow is right. A small room of people is all that is needed to link us personally to the eyewitnesses. No leap is necessary.

Eyewitnesses were the first rememberers. The gospel and letter writers were either eyewitnesses or early hearers of eyewitness reports who wisely created a strong bond between oral and written testimony that could pass across deserts and seas and on into the future. Confident knowledge of the event of the resurrection could pass through time and space by human links of people trusting each other's memories with the additional support of the New Testament as a memory aid. A testimonial succession of rememberers could reach through the centuries to us. To reach us, only twenty or so trustworthy and non-gullible people are all that is needed.

One of Christianity's modern intellectual problems is that academic society has done much to downgrade the authority of eyewitnesses and responsible hearsay witnesses, both in oral and written form. Modern education enjoys teaching distrust; however, this academic romance with doubting hinders our ability to listen well and trust responsibly—especially when dealing with an extraordinary alleged event such as the resurrection. An influential academic source for downgrading the authority

---

60. What follows was first published as Kennedy, "Remembering the Resurrection."
61. Berry, *Jayber Crow*, 353.

of historical testimony is John Locke, who took upon himself what he thought was a sober duty to downplay what he believed was the overly-optimistic trust in witnesses and hearsay evidence presented in the most popular logic textbook of the era: *The Port-Royal Logic*. This textbook, also called *The Art of Thinking*, was extraordinarily popular for two hundred years and offered several arguments supporting the reasonableness of trusting reports of the resurrection of Jesus and later miracles in church history. Locke thought *The Port-Royal Logic* to be too naïve. He worried that it encouraged gullibility. He did not want to undermine people's faith in the historical Jesus; he wanted to emphasize the weaknesses of trusting eyewitness testimony passed down through history.

This story gets complicated by the way both *The Port-Royal Logic* and John Locke looked to mathematics to help their arguments. *The Port-Royal Logic* was famous for introducing mathematical probabilities into decision-making—especially to support the reasonableness of Christianity. In order to encourage trust in historical facts, *The Port-Royal Logic* used the example of the way a deed of land comes down through time. A copy of a deed is signed by two notaries who attest that the copy maintains the information of an original. Since it is highly improbable that the notaries would be lying or bad at their job (the improbability, says the book, would be something like 999 to 1), it is mathematically reasonable to assume that the deeds contain correct facts.[62] The principal facts in documents and copies of documents passed through time and attested by conscientious people along the way should be trusted—the mathematical improbability of error or deceit should give us confidence.

John Locke, however, in his *Essay Concerning Human Understanding*, chose to respond by presenting an alternative mathematics. He presented a sobering formula for diminishing credibility of historical reports. It is good to read Locke's exact words on this: "any testimony, the farther off it is from the original truth, the less force and proof it has." An eyewitness is credible, "but if another equally credible, do witness it from his report, the testimony is weaker; and a third that attests the hear-say of an hearsay, is yet less considerable. So that *in traditional truths, each remove weakens the force of the proof*. And the more hands the tradition has successively passed through, the less strength and evidence does it receive

---

62. Arnauld and Nicole, *Logic or the Art of Thinking*, IV.15.

from them."⁶³ Against the Port-Royal authors, Locke, using mathematical analogies, asserted that information, at every stage of being passed on, becomes proportionally less credible. Locke extended this formula to both oral and written testimony. As for deeds and copies of deeds, "the farther still it is from the original, the less valid it is, and has always less force."⁶⁴

The Port-Royal Logic had emphasized the credibility of historical reports coming down through history through a chain of people. John Locke, on the other hand, emphasized the weakness of historical reports and went so far as to create the rudiments of a mathematical formula for steadily diminishing credibility. Ten years after Locke published his *Essay*, a theologian named John Craig tried to develop a more exact Lockean formula for the diminishing credibility of New Testament history. In his *Mathematical Principles of Christian Theology* (1699), Craig proposed an exact proportion of diminishing credibility and concluded that the New Testament story of the resurrection would have zero credibility in the year 3150.

Throughout the eighteenth and nineteenth centuries, there was much academic debate about mathematical analogies for the credibility of historical testimony, but in the long run of American schools and culture, Locke's position won. It became standard in our schools to emphasize the weakness of testimony—especially the diminishing credibility of historical reports passed down through time. Although Locke wrote about this in terms of mathematicians and probability, his ideas have mostly come to be taught as common sense. Although the American practice of economic and contract law teaches the confidence in deeds and oaths attested by notaries through time, it has become common to teach distrust and diminishing credibility for history. "Come to history as a doubter," says the teacher. In general, our forward-looking culture has enjoyed diminishing the hold that the past has on us.

For Christians, however, it behooves us to remind ourselves that the past presented in the gospels is not too long ago and not too far away. We Christians have erringly been caught up in John Locke's sobering attempts to undermine the confidence taught in *The Port Royal Logic*. We have become accustomed to teaching the image of a "leap" of faith, of jumping a chasm, rather than the more prosaic image of simply conscientiously passing on what has been passed to us. We have too easily fallen

---

63. Locke, *Essay Concerning Human Understanding*, IV.xvi.11.
64. Ibid., IV.xvi.11.

into John Locke's seemingly mathematical reasonableness that says that credibility diminishes proportionally through time.

The nice thing about Jayber Crow's historical insight in Wendell Berry's novel is that it bridges the gap between both *The Port-Royal Logic* and John Locke's *Essay*. Even if you agree with Locke and think historical credibility diminishes in proportion to the number of people it passes through, Jayber Crow points out that the story of Jesus only has to pass through twenty or so people to get to you and me. Credibility can't have diminished that much even by this time. On the other hand, if you think of twenty or so people who have attested like a notary to the basic facts of the written gospel story, we can claim, at minimum, the confidence of a real estate deed coming down to us through time.

My grandmother a few years ago gave me a Griswold #8 frying pan when she was packing to move into a place where she would not have to cook. She told me that my grandfather gave that frying pan to her on their first Christmas together. She was born in 1911 and the pan would have been given in 1931. I am forty-four years old now and my kids are not yet in high school. If I pass that frying pan and story on to a future grandchild, that pan and true story could easily still be passed on almost two centuries after the fact, having only gone through two people: me and my grandchild. A good and true story can be easily carried over hundreds of years by just a few people who want to tell a true story. To help my memory, my grandmother also wrote down the story. Even if my memory of the story gets fuzzy, I can attest to her written testimony as what she had initially told me. As Christians founded upon the historical fact of the resurrection of Jesus, we only need twenty or so conscientious people linked through time to give us the confidence of listening to the eyewitnesses. And to give us greater confidence, we have written attestations that have been passed along to keep the testimony on track.

Jayber Crow is not offering a Christian apologetic; he is simply meditating on how history is close and personal. Our schools want to make history too hard. They want us to over-think it by half. Jayber is not promoting gullibility. He stands in the Classical tradition of knowing history, that history is linked to us by humans. John, who stood at the base of the cross, calls to us in his first letter to trust him as a testifier to what he has seen, heard, and touched so that we can have fellowship with him.[65]

---

65. 1 John 1:1–3.

Mount Darwin

He calls not from long ago and far away, but only from across a small room of friends and family.

"Daunting," commented Dave as the four of us stood at the shore of Blue Heaven Lake (elevation 11,821′) looking up to the top of Mount Darwin. He scrambled around the lake and checked out the area, but it was clear we were not going further. We should have been at the lake an hour earlier to make a real attempt at the peak. This was as high as we were going.

Rick, Steven, and Mount Darwin

Steven had been walking slower and slower. He did not stop nor complain, but he was obviously having trouble. At the time, I thought coming from sea level to almost 12,000 feet in two days had taken the spunk out of him. A few months later, my wife took him to the doctor and found that he has a non-working thyroid. Look at his puffy cheeks in the picture in chapter three. It was amazing he got as far as he did.

With Steven moving slowly, we still had over ten miles to go to get back to the car. Dave and I stood for what seemed a long time looking at the mountain. The guidebook and website I had consulted recommended skirting the southern edge of the lake, then traversing northwest up to the saddle visible in the picture of Steve and me. Once on the saddle, we were to follow the ridge southwesterly to the top. I stood looking, walking the route with my eyes. Dave could have made a solo scramble, made the top, and caught up with us. He is a healthy, hard-charging guy. But Dave has a high sense of responsibility. He and I are teachers, and teachers think in groups. We were here at the perfect starting point on a perfect day, but we were constrained by love.

The success of the trip in my mind was dependent upon standing firmly on the two legs of reasonableness on the summit of Mount Darwin. Reason and testimony, individual responsibility and communal trust, science and the Bible would be grounded on rock. I would be able to look over onto Mendel and across to Spencer, Huxley, and Fiske and entwine understanding with experience. I would have been like John Muir who climbed a tree to understand a storm.

But love supersedes. The boys were at the center of this trek. I wanted to get them to the top, but they were more important to me than the top. I wasn't frustrated with Steven. I was actually overwhelmed with love for the boy. Richard Dawkins, who is sure that Mount Improbable has an easy back route, became famous with a book titled *The Selfish Gene* (1976). He put himself at the bold forefront of a modern version of Spencer's "Social Darwinism" that finds the tap root of social life in competition for resources. Love, especially love of children, as their theory goes, has to actually be a manifestation of genetic selfishness.

There is a book called *The Evolution of Altruism and the Ordering of Love* (1994), by a Roman Catholic theologian interested in sociobiology. He advocates a revived version of Thomas Aquinas' theology about human nature and love because modern sociobiology seems to be pointing in that direction. His book is good in that it is one of the jobs of theologians to make speculative attempts at uniting, under limited conditions, the innovative ideas of an offshoot science with one of the theological traditions well-accepted in Christianity. The book is generally sober but tentatively optimistic for a fruitful interplay of ideas. This seems to me to be good theology and good science at work. The author, Stephen J. Pope, is not abdicating his responsibilities. A traditional service of academics is to be provocative. Theologians, scientists, and even historians should take risks and encourage people to think in new ways or in old ways with new information. But reasonableness supports humility. We should not be overly confident.

Christians often insist on too many things. The Bible tells us there is only one absolutely critical thing: the life, death, and resurrection of Jesus as a historical event. Peter, at Pentecost in a crowded room where amazing things were happening, stood up and did not lead a discussion of the meaning and proper use of speaking in tongues. He did not lead the group in worship songs full of vague theistic aspiration. Rather, he gave a history lesson:

> Men of Israel, listen to this: Jesus of Nazareth was a man accredited by God to you by miracles, wonders and signs, which God did among you through him, as you yourselves know. This man was handed over to you by God's set purpose and foreknowledge, and you, with the help of wicked men, put him to death by nailing him to the cross. But God raised him from the dead, freeing him from the agony of death because it was impossible for death to keep its hold on him.... "Therefore, let all Israel be assured of this: God has made Jesus, whom you crucified, both Lord and Christ."[66]

Peter declared this at a gathering not too long after the meeting of one hundred and twenty disciples who were given the job of finding a new twelfth apostle to replace Judas Iscariot. The one stated criterion for the job was to be an eyewitness. If this good news was going to hit the road and go out into all the world, the twelfth apostle needed "to be a witness with us of his resurrection."[67]

Some things in history you either accept or you don't. You either trust the person reporting or you don't. Herodotus is the founder of our modern discipline of history largely because he made inquiries and kept

---

66. Acts 2:22–24, 36.
67. Acts 1:22.

his readers informed about the strengths and weaknesses of his sources and conclusions. There is a critical moment in his history of the Persian Empire when he gives the gist in translation of a sophisticated discussion of political theory between three leaders who were reforming the Persian government. Herodotus writes: "There are those in Greece who are not convinced of the authenticity of the speeches that were delivered there, but they did take place."[68] You either accept it or you don't.

Matt Repelling

---

68. Herodotus, *Histories*, III.80.

Mount Darwin

Once it was clear that we were not going to climb any further, Matt asked if we could do some rock climbing. I had brought the gear. Shouldn't we at least have some fun with it? He was right. We had some time, and it would be fun.

For harnesses, Matt and I relied on thirty feet of tubular webbing tied as a seat harness. Most climbers use production harnesses, but I trust a well-tied knot more than production buckles. I believe buckles make people over-confident. Knots are usually better (more friction), and people tend to distrust them—so they keep checking them. *Seven Summits* (1986) tells the story of Marty Hoey, who fell to her death on Mount Everest during an attempt to become the first American woman to the top:

> The weather was deteriorating and we could see the others only intermittently through the mist. I heard a call down from above for more rope, and I was just moving to put my pack on when Marty said, "Let me get out of your way." Then I heard this rattling of carabiners and I looked over to see her falling backwards. She grabbed for the fixed rope but couldn't quite reach it. She really gathered speed and then was gone. I looked back and saw her jumar still attached to the rope and to it her open harness, just hanging there. I guess she didn't loop the belt back through the buckle, and it pulled through when she leaned back. I'm sure she went the whole way, 6,000 feet of vertical.[69]

Life or death are often in the little things. I prefer knots to buckles.

Matt, Dave, and I had some fun for an hour rappelling and climbing. Steve took some pictures of us, but didn't want to join the fun. He was happy not to be climbing. Soon we gathered up our gear and started back down to base camp. We had a long way back to the car and an even longer way back to San Diego. I wasn't sure the car would start, let alone get us home.

---

69. Bass, et. al., *Seven Summits*, 67.

5

Homeward

WE DID NOT MAKE it to the top of Mount Darwin. No story of triumph here, intellectual or physical. The story is one of companionship and recognition of academic strengths and weaknesses. Christianity's intellectual foundation—the miracle of Jesus' resurrection—is weak at universities. It is weak in the way ancient human history is a weak academic discipline. Both depend on social methods of knowledge. Being weak, however, does not mean wrong.

There is a story of Peter in the sixth chapter of John where some of the disciples desert Jesus because of hard teachings. Other disciples are grumbling, and Jesus upbraids them: "Does this offend you?" He then turned to his core twelve and asks, "You do not want to leave too, do you?" Peter answered, "Lord, to whom shall we go? You have the words of eternal life." Peter's answer is not full of triumph; it recognizes that our hope is in weakness, the weakness of words from one who, himself, became weak.

Tomorrow morning all four of us will be back in our classrooms where, as students and teachers, we engage in similar companionship and recognition of relative strengths and weaknesses. Classrooms are where we learn rationality, but there is also the higher hope for learning broader, vaguer, principles of reasonableness. Dave and I teach ancient world history, a rather hodge-podge and wimpy subject where the straight lines and generalizations break down and our only hope is in the crooked lines and inconsistencies of listening to words from dead people. Ancient history has no hope in academic rationalism. Where else can it go but to cling to reasonableness? Ancient history accepts the reality of paradox, inconsistency, and human weakness. History recognizes that truths can be unsuccessful, that tragedy and irony often prevail, that what is quirky and odd can be more influential than what is respected and normal.

Homeward

Natural history is rational. It is powerful. But should its confidence wash over into history, negating the quirky fact that we have strong eyewitness and hearsay testimony that Jesus rose from the dead? Is natural history so powerful with its inferences drawn from observation that it has veto power over facts learned from ancient sources?

There is a rational argument that destroys our historical knowledge of Jesus. I have an academic friend who grants that eyewitnesses experienced the resurrected Jesus, but then he says that seeing the resurrected Jesus doesn't mean they actually saw the resurrected Jesus. "The critical issue," he wrote to me in an email, "is whether credibility extends to the truth of their claims or only to the truth of their reports." I grant him his point. Seeing Jesus doesn't mean Jesus is being seen. By extension: when Peter, on top of the mountain, heard God tell him to listen to Jesus, Peter may actually have been listening to himself tell himself to listen to himself.

It is a tricky argument, and Greekish academic traditions always allow for the truth of the tricky. At its core, the argument undermines human perception of anything. Can any of us know anything? Can any of us get outside of our own minds to know anything outside of our brains? Is it possible for a creator God to actually communicate or act in a way we humans could confidently assert as true? What is a scientist observing when he observes something? His or her own mind?

Ancient Greeks enjoyed conundrums and circular reasoning such as, "All that I know is that I know nothing." Our minds can tie us in knots. Greek rationalism is wise to always allow for the tricky. Greek reasonableness is also wise to encourage people not to get bogged down in the tricky. All university disciplines can collapse into a toilet swirl if we allow our minds to play the rationality games that our minds are capable of. Nobody can convince an obstinate skeptic of anything, even the existence of the world around us. All I can say is that I stand in a long Aristotelian and university tradition of optimistic and social reasonableness that offers alternative, practical, maybe-not-fully-persuasive methods of creating credibility for assertions about things we perceive and we believe other people perceive too, now, in the past, and probably into at least the near future. Darwin and I stand together in this tradition.

I follow Peter who listened when God told him to listen to Jesus. Like Peter, my reply to the question of abandoning Jesus is, "To whom shall I go?" Peter recognized that he has to cling to someone or something. There is no personal, independent truth in himself strong enough to save him. Like Peter, I see no hope for me in myself. Like Peter, I cling to words—words communicated with all the limits and frailties of human communication. Worse! Peter at least got to cling to words straight from Jesus. I have to cling to words translated, words written down in Greek, words passed from eyewitnesses through hearsay. Jesus looks at me and asks if I want to leave him like so many others. My answer is that I cling to him through his words as recorded.

I cling to his words in two ways: a church way and a university way. Among the fellowship of believers, I share the tradition and collective experience of two thousand years of believers who, at the core of Christian orthodoxy, believe in the Holy Spirit's oversight over the writing of the whole Bible and that when its authors declare themselves bearing communications from God I must listen as carefully and conscientiously as if Jesus stood with his hand on the shoulder of every author. The Bible is an extension of the incarnation, the stooping down of Truth into mere words. God communicates, but God humbles himself to communicate through chosen authors and helps us, by the power of the Holy Spirit, to read and listen. I believe this in a church way, sharing in a fellowship of prayer and belief. On the other hand, in universities, where the traditional standards of academic disciplines rub against each other, I cling to Jesus' words and deeds as history, as well-attested reports.

History departments, by tradition and common practice, pride themselves in "practical realism" and recognize their "post-heroic situation."[1] We, by traditional rights, have a role in universities as the discipline most oriented to studying human words reporting past events and people. Modern archeology and the social sciences have been developed to avoid the weaknesses of words. However, traditional history is a social study, not a social science. The stronger university disciplines strive to discover things that are independent of the frailties of people. History departments, however, are mired in people, especially the words of dead people.

My dad was a weatherman, a type of natural historian. Everybody laughs at the errors of weathermen. But when my dad predicted the fu-

---

1. Appleby, Hunt, and Jacobs, *Telling the Truth about History*, 247–48.

ture, a fleet of warships immediately changed course. Dad was using history in the form of past measurements to look for patterns that could be turned into probabilities of future events. Meteorology is a field of natural history strong enough to persuade admirals that disbelief is too big a risk. I teach ancient history, a job more laughable than a weatherman's. My job is rooted in, with, and through people. Eighteen-year-old students dismiss my analyses. I can't imagine having the power of argument capable of convincing an admiral to change the course of a fleet.

Natural historians can begin by making observations then move independently to historical assertions and even prediction of the future. Natural history is strong and deserves respect. However, natural history can't tell you about Cleopatra. Archeology and history work very well together, but archeology can't help us understand Julius Caesar's goals and policies. Pick up any freshman history textbook and what distinguishes it from an archeology text is the amount of people that are named, the specific description of events, and, most importantly, phrases such as "Alexander desired..." or "Pope Gregory realized..." or "Although Caesar Augustus presented himself as the savior of the Republic, he was actually ..." Natural history can't credibly offer phrases like those. Historians are needed at the university banquet. No other discipline is methodically devoted to investigating, analyzing, and assessing the thoughts, words, and actions of individual people in the ancient past. No other discipline is as devoted to listening to reports about people and events. Historians cling to these reports. Historians cling to words. It is a precarious position, but it's the basis of the contribution we make to the whole university.

Christianity is rooted in ancient words. God became human and used human words. Paul told the Corinthian church that the foundations of their faith were the words of the eyewitnesses reporting an event. Paul, wanting to ground the Corinthian church's intellectual claims in the Greek culture of his time and place, pointed to an historical event, the resurrection.

We Christians are told to be prepared in our Greek-influenced university-honoring culture "to give the reason for the hope that you have."[2] Paul tells us the foundation for that reason: Jesus' resurrection. Paul reached for the weakest link in comprehensive Greek reasonableness: historical knowledge. Jesus had humbled himself to become human. Jesus humbled himself so much as to have his message embedded in the frailty

---

2. 1 Pet 3:15.

of human words passed among humans over time. He humbled himself to have the intellectual strength of the faith embedded in the weakest of Greek intellectual methods. Jesus rigged Christian apologetics to be weak. Given all this humbling, all this weakness and frailty, Christians should never expect to win debates. Paul did not win in Athens. Christians won't ever win in universities. Our Christian responsibility in universities is to claim our place at the foot of the university table, a place long established for us by the tradition of reasonableness that reaches back to Aristotle.

From Herodotus to the modern historians, the wisest practitioners of our discipline have not tried to pretend to strength. The wisest historians expect good readers to criticize the evidence even after we have shown that it is the best we've got. Barry Cunliffe, in *The Extraordinary Voyage of Pytheas the Greek* (2001), gathers all the bits and pieces of written and archeological evidence for a voyage to Iceland in the generation after Aristotle. Cunliffe's is a beautiful book of common-sense historical pragmatism. We don't have Pytheas' whole book, just pieces quoted in other books. Furthermore, even writers in the ancient world attacked Pytheas' account. But Cunliffe, like the best of historians, walks readers through the range of evidence, opposed and supporting, weak and weaker, and reaches for phrasings like this when promoting the possibility that Pytheas made it all the way to Iceland: "This is clearly an imaginative scenario—a fairy story, perhaps; a product of wishful thinking. Yet, returning firmly to the hard evidence. . . . It seems appropriate to take [Pytheas] at his word."[3] Jesus humbled himself to human history reported in ancient words. This is the resurrection's best foothold in universities.

Extraordinary claims, whether from Pytheas or Luke, always come down to the "hard evidence" and the need to trust someone. It was common for historians in the Roman Empire such as Luke, Josephus, and Eusebius to offer a preface to their book stating their goals and method of research. In essence, each of these authors makes a plea to the reader: "Trust me, I have done the best I can with what I have to give you the truth." In the historical tradition, the reader is then under obligation to read critically while also giving the author the benefit of the doubt.

Having failed to reach the summit of Darwin, we hiked back to our base camp and gathered our gear. Nothing was lighter because food had not

---

3. Cunliffe, *Extraordinary Voyage*, 135.

Homeward

been much of our weight. We talked about coming back next August. Snow would soon block any access until probably the middle of next July.

We shouldered our packs and connected with the trail. It was a beautiful Sunday afternoon in the mountains. We met young couples day-hiking as we picked our way down. They would usually say something encouraging to the boys, who were looking pretty ragged at this point. Back to being single-file on the trail, my mind was free to wander.

I like Charles Darwin. I enjoy the story of his life. He was diligent and disciplined. He was adventurous. I would have enjoyed being on the *Beagle* with him for his five-year circumnavigation.

Robert FitzRoy, captain of the *Beagle*, usually gets treated badly by biologists, but Darwin liked him. Darwin, a rather indifferent young student when he boarded the *Beagle*, probably learned much about self-discipline and precise record-keeping from FitzRoy. It has been common in books and lecture halls to emphasize the progressive intelligence of Darwin by dramatically contrasting him to the supposedly morose Christian fundamentalist who commanded the *Beagle*. Darwin, in the tradition of heroic scientist, must be surrounded by benighted conservatives. The classroom drama of the Darwin-FitzRoy relationship is usually resolved by noting that twenty-five years after the *Beagle's* circumnavigation, FitzRoy tried publicly to debunk Darwin's newly published book *On the Origin of Species* (1859) and eventually killed himself by slitting his throat.

But the standard story is complicated by the fact that Captain FitzRoy was a remarkable scientist himself. He was a high-minded, highly-skilled captain with a mathematical bent that eventually led him to be one of the founders of modern naval meteorology. It was FitzRoy, working for the navy, who first conceived of a system of gathering daily weather data by telegraphs and printing a daily weather forecast in the London newspapers. Throughout his naval career on land and at sea his junior officers honored him and readily volunteered to stay with him. His superiors made sure his talents were not wasted.

At the beginning of the voyage, FitzRoy was twenty-five and Darwin twenty-two. I can picture myself in my early twenties joining in the voyage. The trip was focused on charting the southern tip of South America. FitzRoy chose Darwin partly for companionship and partly because, as he said, he wanted someone to focus on geology and geography while he did hydrography. I suppose FitzRoy could have picked me to help with the dinner conversation. A historian is always useful at the dinner table.

I have looked at schematic drawings of the ship and pictured the dining room full of books, technical instruments, and charts. Imagine long after-dinner conversations at sea with two such keen observers, both driven by so much being unknown about the world. One would become the greatest exponent of our ability to know the deep past, the causes and stages of creation. The other would become the first daily wizard of scientific fortune-telling, a forecaster of weather. The former was an observer-categorizer, the latter a mathematician-modeler.

Me? What would a historian contribute to the table conversation? My responsibility would be to pass on what can't be known by observation or mathematical modeling. I could contribute useful and informative stories, such as the story of Edmond Halley, the sailor-scientist who lived over a hundred years before Darwin and FitzRoy. Halley would be interesting to both my companions. He was a great meteorologist, navigator, and earth scientist. As an astronomer, he used historical modeling to predict the return of what we now call "Halley's Comet." By combining history and math, he predicted the future. Halley was also one of the first people of his era to see the predictive power of statistics. But the best story of Halley, the story most interesting at the dining table of the *HMS Beagle*, would be Halley's three scientific voyages on the relatively small *HMS Paramour*. On the first two voyages, between 1698 and 1700, Halley sailed far into the south and north Atlantic to chart magnetic variations from true north. On the third, he charted tides in the English Channel. Contrary to any naval traditions, the British Admiralty officially commissioned Halley, a forty-year-old secretary to a scientific organization who had never been in the navy, as master and commander of one of his majesty's naval vessels. On one of the first official naval voyages dedicated to scientific purpose, the captain was a scientist! Later, in 1729, when he was poor after retiring from a job as Royal Astronomer, the queen found him a pension as a half-pay naval post captain.

Historians are good for stories like that. Darwin and FitzRoy would have laughed at the absurdity of creating a navy captain out of a middle-aged scientist. It is one of our duties as historians to keep alive true stories of laughable absurdities.

I like to think that Darwin would have liked me. I like him. He would have recognized that my job as a historian allows me to focus on the validity of absurdly odd reported events. On the other hand, I would have recognized his need to throw out the absurd and quirky so as to focus

Homeward

on general laws. When FitzRoy and I would have agreed about using the Bible for history, Darwin would have probably thought both of us naive; I think we could have had great dinner-table debates and conversations. I like to think that the three of us would have enjoyed and appreciated each other.

FitzRoy later killed himself. His family had a history of suicide. Darwin was later devastated by the death of his young daughter and his family had no history of trusting God in times of crisis. Both men had a tendency toward melancholy. They found solace in silence and hard work. It is a mystery to me why I feel so much divine grace in my life. Why didn't God shower some extra grace on FitzRoy and Darwin? Maybe God did. I don't know. It would have been nice to sail with them. I wish for both of them that things had turned out better.

One thing Darwin and Christianity agree upon is the naturalness of selfishness and death. Christianity and evolution are rooted in the reality of violent competition, suffering, pain, and death. Christianity does not absolve God of the ultimate responsibility for allowing suffering, pain, and death. All Christians can say in the face of such things is that God as Jesus joined us in the suffering and pain and saves us by his death and resurrection. Darwin helped scientifically understand the integral role suffering and death play in natural history. Christianity affirms the integral depth of suffering and pain in human life. God punished humanity with suffering and death and offered redemption to all in his own suffering and death.

Our pace back to the car was quicker than it was going up. We each gained energy as the oxygen thickened. Gravity was also working for us rather than against us. We didn't talk much. We were deep in our own thoughts. A few hours and a little over ten miles later, we dropped to the pavement below Lake Sabrina. I sped up ahead of the group because I was anxious to see if the car would start.

Gravity is a wonder. Aristotle thought of gravity as being guided by a purpose. Gravity drew things to where they should be. Isaac Newton pushed the idea of gravity as an impersonal "force," but admitted that the term "force" may mean something occult or spiritual. Nowadays we find it helpful to use the term "field," and have a much greater understanding of the workings and complexities of gravity. Gravity, however, is still a wonder.

I take heart that several of the Darwinists whose names are associated with the mountains behind me thought that gravity was both a law and something under the influence of spirits. Alfred Wallace believed in the truth of reported instances of levitation. Mounts Wallace, Haeckel, Lamark, and Mendel are named after men who believed in spiritual powers. Theodore Solomons came from a family of spiritualists. The mountains above Evolution Valley honor people open to all kinds of ideas and willing to follow evidence wherever it led. There were many academic spiritualists in that generation. They had open minds to that which academics before and after them refused to even entertain.

In 1906, Josiah P. Quincy, a grandson of a president of Harvard and a mayor of Boston, told a story reported in the Proceedings of the Massachusetts Historical Society. Quincy remembered sitting with his grandfather in the 1840s midst a gathering of distinguished Boston university men. The men proceeded to smirk at the old Puritan belief in spiritual powers. Young Quincy listened and, some sixty years later, thought his elders a bit narrow-minded. "Men of that time," he wrote, "failed to understand that what they regarded as supernatural might be an obscure part of nature which could be brought into organic touch with other experiences which make up life. The great generalization we call Evolution offers us a comprehensive outlook which was denied to them." Quincy went on to quote John Fiske and cite Ernst Haeckel. Like Theodore Solomons, Quincy saw Fiske, Haeckel, and Wallace as men who opened modern minds to the possibility of "supernormal" spiritualism. Of Alfred Wallace, Quincy wrote: "the eminent naturalist, expert in biology and physiology, possessed of those powers of careful observation which will forever associate his name with that of Darwin,... tells us that he has seen a chair with its occupant ascend 'in broad daylight.'"[4]

Quincy and Wallace believed in the law of gravity, but the law of gravity did not wash throughout their thinking so much that they could not believe reports of individual instances where the law did not apply. For Quincy it was the theory of evolution that had opened his generation's eyes to this. His grandfathers' generation was so rational that it lost the ability to believe such reports.

---

4. Quincy, "Cotton Mather," 446.

Homeward

Reports of miracles, especially Jesus' resurrection, are the central problem. Should ancient historians believe reports of wild events, even really wild events? Many would say no, but I fear their perspective arises as much out of personal insecurities as insistent rationalism. Christians in universities need to be willing to play the fool if for no other reason than that the fool is often the person with the most open mind.

There is another reason some people insist that the ancients were wrong about miracles. They want to protect God. Michael Ruse, in *Can A Darwinian Be A Christian?* (2000), writes as a philosopher who can find plenty of ways for Christians to tweak Christianity so as to fit with Darwinian truth. But Ruse is befuddled by insistence on biblically reported miracles. Ruse thinks an emphasis on miracles is an intellectual cop-out. Most importantly, Ruse thinks Christians who believe in miracles demean God. Such a theology is undignified, and God is turned into "a conjuror," a magician, a circus act. Would a serious God do tricks?[5] Would a serious God meddle with the weather, kill a tree, walk on water, and supply wine at weddings? Would the God worthy of rational people do those weird appearing/disappearing tricks before levitating himself up into the clouds? Such a God is not worthy of a sober and sophisticated Christianity.

This is where we start and end with this academic excursion into the differences between natural history and ancient history. The God of traditional, biblical, ancient history is not a serious God. The God of ancient history is an irritating God who is self-humbled into an irritating but reliably true story. The historical God is a conjuror, a magician, a disconcertingly undignified God who can be dismissed as a circus act. Paul associated God with the wacky gods of the Greeks. I don't defend God; I follow God. If I don't praise God the rocks will; Mount Darwin, itself, will praise God. If I abandon the irritating history, to what would I turn? To Ruse's sober and rational God? To the wimpy God of so many modern theologians influenced by Darwinism, a God who is not sovereign creator, who cannot act or communicate decisively, who is responsible for love, but not suffering and pain? I am too much a historian to think that a Darwinian God is anything other than something Darwinians made up.

---

5. Ruse, *Can a Darwinian Be a Christian*, 97.

Jesus, History, and Mount Darwin

Theodore Solomons named the mountains behind me to honor men who felt empowered by Darwin to pursue deeper into the workings of nature. What inspired many people about Wallace, and probably inspired Solomons when he heard Wallace speak in San Francisco, was the great evolutionist's honest reporting of evidences of unexplainable powers that seemed unbounded by natural laws.

I am intrigued by Wallace for this reason too. I have never seen anyone levitate in a chair, but I believe multiple well-attested reports of a man walking on water. Does this disqualify me as a university man? Maybe it does by the standards of some of the severe rationalists, *Totalizers*, who want to reshape the future of universities. On the other hand, universities do not have an officially sanctioned orthodoxy. The university thrives as a collection of disciplines using many methods of inquiry and understanding. Yet, there is the long Aristotelian tradition of universities as places of tentative investigation. Universities are a gathering of tinkerers under an umbrella of a reasonableness that is negotiated through hundreds of years of tradition based on the variety of tools available in the university pocketknife. If we understand that disciplines have mutually independent reasonable methods, each proposing credible conclusions, then it is reasonable to think that gravity is a natural law and Jesus walked on water. Darwin can be right about the normal functioning of a mechanism of variation and selection, while Jesus' resurrection can point to God who is active and communicating in human history. Natural history can do its good work and ancient history can do its good work. Neither is subservient to the other. One is scientifically and rationally stronger than the other, but the weaker has its academic strengths too.

My diesel engine struggled all the way back to San Diego. On the high desert we kept to the speed limit while listening to the second game of the World Series on the radio. But as we climbed over the mountains north of San Bernardino, the car was straining to go forty miles an hour. A couple of hours later, dropping finally into Mission Valley and the flatlands of the San Diego River, our top speed was around fifty miles an hour. In Ocean Beach, we found Dave's old convertible VW. It was close to midnight with school in the morning for all of us. The boys and I had one last hill to climb to get home on top of the ridge of Point Loma. I asked Dave to follow me up to make sure we got there. He did, and my car soon whimpered to a stop in front of my house. Dave waved goodbye as I began to unload the boys' packs from the roof rack.

Afterword

Because this is a book about historical reliability, I should tell you that all the events reported here happened. The motivation for the trip was to get to the top for the purpose stated. Given a historically reliable framework, the thoughts in the book were reconstructed, elaborated, and edited off and on over the course of a few years.

David Nieman, Rebecca Flietstra, Kara deFreitas, Walt Gustufson, Sam Powell, Jim Meals, Doug Webster, Jeff Cann, and Darrel Falk were especially helpful and supportive. Kaitlin Barr, a student in my World Civilizations class, edited the final draft. Folk at Point Loma Nazarene University and the First Presbyterian Church, San Diego remain consistently supportive. The problem with the car proved to be only bad diesel clogging the injectors.

Bibliography

Andrews, E. C. "First Ascent of Mount Darwin—1908." *Sierra Club Bulletin* XII.1 (1924) 87–90.
Appleby, Joyce, Lynn Hunt, and Margaret Jacobs. *Telling the Truth About History.* New York: W. W. Norton, 1995.
Archer, Léonie J., et al. *Women in Ancient Societies: An Illusion of the Night.* New York: Routledge, 1994.
Aristotle. *The Art of Rhetoric.* Translated by H. C. Lawson-Tancred. New York: Penguin Classics, 1991.
———. *Topica.* Translated by W. A. Pickard-Cambridge. Vol. 1. *The Works of Aristotle.* Oxford: Clarendon Press, 1928.
Arnauld, Antoine and Pierre Nicole. *Logic or the Art of Thinking.* Edited by Jill Vance Buroker. Cambridge: Cambridge University Press, 1996.
Augustine. *On Christian Doctrine.* Translated by J.F.Shaw. Ser 1, vol. 3. *Nicene and Post-Nicene Fathers.* Edited by Philip Schaff. Grand Rapids, MI: Eerdmans, 1988.
Ayers, Robert H. "C. S. Peirce On Miracles." *Transactions of the Charles S. Peirce Society* 16 (1980) 242–54.
Bahrani, Zainaab. *Women of Babylon: Gender and Representation in Ancient Mesopotamia.* London: Routledge, 2001.
Barnes, Timothy D. *Constantine and Eusebius.* Cambridge: Harvard University Press, 1981.
Bass, Dick, et. al. *Seven Summits.* New York: Warner Books, 1986.
Bauckham, Richard. *Jesus and the Eyewitnesses: The Gospels as Eyewitness Testimony.* Grand Rapids, MI: Eerdmans, 2006.
Beaulieu, Paul-Alain. "King Nabonidus and the Neo-Babylonian Empire." In *Civilizations of the Ancient Near East.* Edited by Jack M. Sasson. Peabody, MA: Hendrickson, 2001.
Beckwith, Francis J. *David Hume's Argument Against Miracles: A Critical Analysis.* Lanham, MD: University Press of America, 1989.
Berlinski, David. *The Advent of the Algorithm: The Idea that Rules the World.* New York: Harcourt, 2000.
Berry, Wendell. *Jayber Crow.* Washington D.C.: Counterpoint, 2000.
Blomberg, Craig. *The Historical Reliability of the Gospels.* Downers Grove, IL: InterVarsity, 1987.
Burnham, Robert, et. al. *A Guide to Backyard Astronomy.* San Francisco: Fog City Press, 1997.
Burns, R. M. *The Great Debate on Miracles: From Joseph Glanville to David Hume.* Lewisburg: Bucknell University, 1981.
Burridge, R.A. *What Are the Gospels?* Cambridge: Cambridge University Press, 1992.

Bibliography

Carter, Bill and Merrie Sue Carter. *Latitude: How American Astronomers Solved the Mystery of Variation.* Annapolis: Naval Institute Press, 2002.

Casson, Lionel. *The Ancient Mariners: Seafarers and Sea Fighters of the Mediterranean in Ancient Times.* 2nd ed. Princeton: Princeton University Press, 1991.

Chesterton, Gilbert Keith. *St. Thomas Aquinas: The "Dumb Ox."* Garden City, NY: Image Books, 1956.

Cicero. *De Oratore.* Translated by E. W. Sutton. Cambridge, Mass.: Harvard University Press, 1959.

Coady, C. A. J. *Testimony: A Philosophical Study.* Oxford: Oxford University Press, 1992.

Cohn, Norman. *Noah's Flood: The Genesis Story in Western Thought.* New Haven: Yale University Press, 1996.

Collingwood, R. G. *The Idea of History.* Oxford: Clarendon Press, 1946.

Craige, John. *John Craige's Mathematical Principles of Christian Theology.* Edited and introduced by Richard Nash. Carbondale, IL: Southern Illinois University Press, 1988.

Cunliffe, Barry. *The Extraordinary Voyage of Pytheas the Greek.* New York: Penguin, 2001.

Darwin, Charles. *On the Origin of the Species: A Facsimile of the First Edition.* Cambridge: Harvard University, 1964.

———. *The Voyage of the Beagle.* Santa Barbara: The Narrative Press, 2001.

Daston, Lorraine. *Classical Probability in the Enlightenment.* Princeton: Princeton University Press, 1988.

Dawkins, Richard. *Climbing Mount Improbable.* New York: W. W. Norton, 1996.

———. *The Selfish Gene.* New York: Oxford University Press, 1976.

Dawson, Glen. "Mountain-Climbing on the 1933 Outing." *Sierra Club Bulletin* XIX no. 3 (1934) 92–95.

Dembski, William. *Intelligent Design: The Bridge Between Science and Theology.* Downers Grove, IL: InterVarsity, 1999.

Dennett, Daniel C. *Darwin's Dangerous Idea: Evolution and the Meanings of Life.* New York: Simon & Schuster, 1995.

Desmond, Adrien and James Moore. *Darwin: The Life of a Tormented Evolutionist.* New York: W. W. Norton, 1991.

DeYoung, Donald B. *Astronomy and Creation.* St. Joseph, MO: Creation Research Society Books, 1995.

———. *Astronomy and the Bible: Questions and Answers.* Second ed. Grand Rapids, MI: Baker Books, 2000.

Dillery, John. "Darius and the Tomb of Nitocris (Hdt. I.187)." *Classical Philology* 87 (1992) 31.

Eusebius. *The History of the Church.* Translated by G. A. Williamson. New York: Penguin Classics, 1989.

———. *The Reply . . . to the work of Philostratus on Apollonius.* Vol. 3 of *Philostratus.* Translated by Christopher P. Jones. Cambridge: Loeb Classical Library, 2006.

Evans, J.A.S. "Individuals in Herodotus." *Herodotus, Explorer of the Past: Three Essays.* Princeton, NJ: Princeton University, 1991. 41–88.

Fehling, Detlev. *Herodotus and His "Sources": Citation, Invention, and Narrative Art.* Translated by J. G. Howie. Leeds, UK: Francis Cairns, 1989.

Fischer, David Hackett. *Historians' Fallacies: Toward a Logic of Historical Thought.* New York: Harper & Row, 1970.

Fiske, John. *Excursions of an Evolutionist.* Boston: Houghton Mifflin, 1883.

Bibliography

———. *Outlines of Cosmic Philosophy: based on the doctrine of evolution with criticisms on the positive philosophy.* London: Macmillan, 1874.

———."The Jesus of History." *The Unseen World, and Other Essays.* 15th ed. Boston: Houghton, Mifflin and Co., 1876.

Gould, Stephen. *Rocks of Ages: Science and Religion in the Fullness of Life.* New York: Ballantine, 1999.

Grafton, Anthony and Megan Williams. *Christianity and the Transformation of the Book: Origen, Eusebius, and the Library of Caesarea.* Cambridge: Harvard University Press, 2006.

Hacking, Ian. *The Emergence of Probability.* Cambridge: Cambridge University Press, 1975.

Haeckel, Ernst. *The Riddle of the Universe.* Translated by Joseph McCabe. Buffalo, NY: Promethius Books, 1992.

Henig, Robin Marantz. *The Monk in the Garden: The Lost and Found Genius of Gregor Mendel the Father of Genetics.* Boston: Houghton Mifflin, 2000.

Herodotus. *The Histories.* Translated by Robin Wakefield. Introduction and notes by Carolyn Dewald. Oxford, Oxford University, 1998.

Hofstadter, Richard. *Social Darwinism in American Thought.* New York: George Braziller, 1959.

Hume, David. *Enquiries Concerning Human Understanding.* 3rd ed. Edited by P.H. Nidditch. Oxford: Clarendon Press, 1975.

Huxley, Thomas H."On the Advisableness of Improving Natural Knowledge."*Autobiography and Selected Essays.* Reprint of 1909 edition. McLean, VA: IndyPublish.com, n.d.

Jacobs, David M. *Secret Life: Firsthand Accounts of UFO Abductions.* New York: Simon & Schuster, 1992.

Kennedy, Rick. "The Application of Mathematics to Christian Apologetics in Pascal's *Pensées* and Arnauld's *The Port-Royal Logic.*" *Fides et Historia* 23 (1991) 37–52.

———. "Faith and History: A Better Understanding of Balancing Likelihoods." *Fides et Historia* 29 (1997) 66–73.

———. *A History of Reasonableness: Testimony and Authority in the Art of Thinking.* Rochester, NY: University of Rochester Press, 2004.

———."Miracles in the Dock: A Critique of the Historical Profession's Special Treatment of Alleged Spiritual Events." *Fides et Historia* 26 (1994) 7–22.

———."Remembering the Resurrection." *Modern Reformation.* 13:2 (March/April, 2004) 40–42, 47.

Kidger, Mark. *The Star of Bethlehem.* Princeton: Princeton University Press, 1999.

Kline, Morris. *Mathematics: The Loss of Certainty.* New York: Oxford University, 1980.

Kuhrt, Amélie."The Ancient Near East in Western Thought." In *Civilizations of the Ancient Near East.* Edited by Jack M. Sasson. Peabody, MA: Hendrickson, 2001.

———."Non-Royal Women in the Late Babylonian Period: A Survey." In *Women's Earliest Records: From Ancient Egypt and Western Asia.* Edited by Barbara S. Lesko. Atlanta: Scholars Press, 1989.

LeConte, Joseph. *The Autobiography of Joseph LeConte.* New York: Appleton, 1903.

———. *Evolution, Its Nature, Its Evidences, and Its Relation to Religious Thought.* New York: Appleton, 1897.

———. *A Journal of Ramblings Through the High Sierras of California.* Yosemite National Park: Yosemite Association, 1994.

Bibliography

Levine, Michael P. *Hume and the Problem of Miracles: A Solution.* Boston: Kluwer Academic Publishers, 1989.

Locke, John. *An Essay Concerning Human Understanding.* Edited by Peter H. Nidditch. Oxford: Clarendon Press, 1987.

Luraghi, Nino. *The Historian's Craft in the Age of Herodotus.* New York: Oxford University, 2001.

Marius, Richard. *A Short Guide to Writing About History.* 3rd ed. New York: Longman, 1999.

Marincola, John. *Authority and Tradition in Ancient Historiography.* Cambridge, UK: Cambridge University Press, 1997.

McDonough, Tom. "Star Stuff." *Skeptic* 4 no. 4 (1996) 10–17.

McPhee, John. *Assembling California.* New York: Farrar, Straus, and Giroux, 1993.

———. *Rising from the Plains.* New York: Farrar, Straus and Giroux, 1986.

Merrill, Kenneth R. "Hume's 'Of Miracles,' Peirce, and the Balancing of Likelihoods." *Journal of the History of Ideas.* 29 (1991) 85–113.

Miller, Kenneth R. *Finding Darwin's God: A Scientist's Search for Common Ground Between God and Evolution.* New York: HarperCollins, 1999.

Montgomery, John Warwick. *History and Christianity.* Downers Grove, IL: InterVarsity, 1964.

———. *The Quest for Noah's Ark: a treasury of documented accounts from ancient times to the present day of sightings of the ark & explorations of Mount Ararat with a narration of the author's successful ascent to the summit of Noah's mountain.* Minneapolis, Bethany Fellowship, 1972.

Newman, John Henry. *The Idea of the University.* New York: Longmans, Green and Co., 1910.

Peirce, Charles S. "A Preliminary Chapter, Toward an Examination of Hume's Argument Against Miracles, in its Logic and in its History." "Hume's Arguments Against Miracles, and the Idea of Natural Law." "On the Logic of Drawing History from Ancient Documents especially from Testimonies." In *Historical Perspectives on Peirce's Logic of Science.* Edited by Carolyn Eisele. Berlin: Mouton Publishers, 1985, II, 703–801, 890–913.

Pelling, Christopher. *Plutarch and History.* Swansea: Classical Press of Wales, 2002.

Penrose, Roger. *The Road to Reality: A Complete Guide to the Laws of the Universe.* New York: Knopf, 2004.

Philostratus. *The Life of Apollonius of Tyana.* Vols 1–2 of *Philostratus.* Translated by Christopher P. Jones. Cambridge: Loeb Classical Library, 2006.

Pirsig, Robert M. *Zen and the Art of Motorcycle Maintenance: an inquiry into values.* New York: Morrow, 1974.

Polybius, *The Rise of the Roman Empire.* Translated by Ian Scott-Kilvert. New York: Penguin Classics, 1979.

Pomeroy, Sarah B. *Women's History and Ancient History.* Chapel Hill, NC: University of North Carolina, 1991.

Pope, Stephen J. *The Evolution of Altruism and the Ordering of Love.* Washington D.C.: Georgetown University Press, 1994.

Quincy, Josiah. "Cotton Mather and the Supernormal in New England History." *Proceedings of the Massachusetts Historical Society* Series II, Vol. XX (1906): 446.

Raby, Peter. *Alfred Russell Wallace: A Life.* Princeton: Princeton University Press, 2001.

Romm, James. *Herodotus.* New Haven: Yale University, 1998.

Bibliography

Romm, James. *Herodotus*. New Haven: Yale University, 1998.

Rowell, Chester. "The Mountain and the Sea." In *Voices of the Earth: A Treasury of the Sierra Club Bulletin*. Edited by Ann Gilliam. San Francisco: Sierra Club Books, 1979.

Ruse, Michael. *Can A Darwinian Be A Christian: The Relationship Between Science and Religion*. Cambridge: Cambridge University Press, 2000.

Sagan, Carl and Thorton Page. *UFO's: A Scientific Debate*. New York: Norton, 1972.

Sanders, N. K. *Epic of Gilgamesh*. New York: Penguin Classics, 1972.

Sargent, Shirley. *Solomons of the Sierra: The Pioneer of the John Muir Trail*. Yosemite, CA: Flying Spur Press, 1989.

Sasson, Jack M. *Civilizations of the Ancient Near East*. 2 vols. New York: Charles Scribner's Sons, 1995.

Secor, R. J. *The High Sierra: Peaks, Passes and Trails*. 2nd ed. Seattle: The Mountaneers, 1999.

Shenk, Dean. "Introduction." In Joseph LeConte's *A Journal of Ramblings Through the High Sierras of California*. Yosemite National Park: Yosemite Association, 1994.

Smith, Edwin. "The Shipwreck According to St. Luke." In *The Rudder Treasury*. Edited by Tom Davin. New York: Sheridan House, 2003. 55–66.

Solomons, Theodore. "The Beginnings of the John Muir Trail." *Sierra Club Bulletin*. 25 no. 1 (February, 1940).

Stephens, Lester. *Joseph LeConte: Gentle Prophet of Evolution*. Baton Rouge: Louisiana State University Press, 1982.

Tacitus. *The Annals of Imperial Rome*. Translated by Michael Grant. New York: Penguin Classics, 1996.

Thoreau, Henry David. *The Maine Woods*. New York: Library of America, 1985.

Thucydides, *The Landmark Thucydides: A Comprehensive Guide to The Peloponnesian War*. Edited by Robert B. Strassler. Translated by Richard Crawley. New York: Touchstone, 1996.

Waters, K. H. "The Importance of Individuals." In *Herodotus the Historian: His Problems, Methods and Originality*. London: Croom Helm, 1985. 136–51.

Winston, George P. *John Fiske*. New York: Twayne, 1972.

Wiseman, Donald J. "Babylonia 605–539 B.C." *Cambridge Ancient History*. 2nd ed. Vol. 3, pt 2. Edited by John Boardman, et. al. Cambridge: Cambridge University Press, 1991.

———. *Nebachadrezzar and Babylon*. Oxford: Oxford University, 1991.

———. "Palace and Temple Gardens in the Ancient Near East." *Monarchies and Socio-Religious Traditions in the Near East: papers read at the 31st International Congress of Human Sciences in Asia and North Africa*. Edited by Takahito Mikasa. Wiesbaden: Harrassowitz, 1984.

Yamauchi, Edwin M. *Persia and the Bible*. Grand Rapids, MI: Baker Books, 1996.

www.ingramcontent.com/pod-product-compliance
Lightning Source LLC
Chambersburg PA
CBHW070504090426
42735CB00012B/2670